March 17 - 2012

Happy Cooking
Sun Valley style

Jeanne
&
Jerry

Entertaining
Sun Valley Style

Behind the Scenes from the
Sun Valley Center Wine Auction

acknowledgements

The Sun Valley Center for the Arts is deeply grateful to the Junior Patrons Circle for conceiving the idea for this book, and for their unwavering commitment to making it a reality.

On behalf of everyone associated with the project, The Center extends special thanks to the generous funders who underwrote the photography, design and editing of the book.

Katherine and Buffalo Rixon
Gail and Jack Thornton
Laura and Hunter Vogel

Thank you to all our recipe testers for their attention to detail and willingness to roll up their sleeves and don their aprons in the pursuit of perfection. Your time at your cutting boards and over your stoves was invaluable.

Kristin Bigelow, Eltiena Campbell, Eric and Christy Giles, Jennifer Goitiandia,
Tracy Lee, Tyra MacGuffie, Nancy Malko, Candice Pate, Katherine Rixon,
Laurie Sammis, Cathy Swink, Peta Verhaeghe and Laura Vogel

The book would not have been possible without the wonderful cooperation of the many chefs who shared the recipes for their inspired creations and the hosts who graciously opened up their stunning homes to us for inclusion in the book.

Of course, the history of the Sun Valley Center Wine Auction has been completely dependent on the marvelous vintners and wineries, too numerous to mention, that have participated over the years. There are not words to adequately describe how grateful we are to you all. Thanks also to Riedel, who has generously contributed to the "All About Wine" section of this book, and to Mark Ervin of Professional Wine Service.

Special thanks go to Judith McQueen for her endless hours in the kitchen and in the studio preparing recipes and styling them to perfection for our numerous studio food photo shoots. And a heartfelt and singular thank you to Paulette Phlipot for her exceptional dedication to the project.

Lastly, Mandala Media, led by Laurie Sammis, deserves enormous credit for channeling all the enthusiasm for this book into a practical plan for creating it. Laurie and her team's expertise in all facets kept the project moving forward and enabled a group with little publishing experience to produce a professional product that looks like we dreamed it would and of which we can all be proud.

And to those of you who purchase this book, thank you as well. Because of your support, thousands of children will benefit from incredible arts and cultural experiences that will nurture their creative potential, expand their horizons and prepare them to face the world with open hearts and minds.

Sun Valley Center for the Arts and its Junior Patrons Circle Committee:
Christy Giles, Sonya Johnston, Tracy Lee, Tyra MacGuffie, Pauli Ochi, Candice Pate,
Katherine Rixon, Laurie Sammis, Peta Verhaeghe, Hunter and Laura Vogel, Tim Wolff

Book design by Mandala Media, a group of artists and editors who collaborate on design and printed book projects.
Compiled and Edited: Laurie Sammis
Art Direction: Robin Leahy
Editor: Mike McKenna
Food Editor: Jessica Holmes
Copy Editor: Carrie Lightner

Cover: Local Heirloom Melon with Duck Prosciutto, see page 23. Photo by Paulette Philpot.

Library of Congress Cataloging-in-Publication data is available on request.

ISBN: 978-0-9834470-0-9
First Edition 2011

Entertaining
Sun Valley Style

Behind the Scenes from the
Sun Valley Center Wine Auction

A compilation by
The Junior Patrons Circle
of the Sun Valley Center for the Arts

Food Photography
Paulette Phlipot
Dev Khalsa

Food Stylist
Judith McQueen

Mandala Media, LLC
Book Publishing Division
www.mandala-media.com

contributors

Guest Chefs

Constantinos "Taki" Laliotitis

Beau MacMillan

Ben Spungin

Cal Stamenov

John Tesar

Sue Zemanick

Local Chefs

CK's Real Food | Chris Kastner and Rebecca Kastner

CIRO Restaurant & Wine Bar | Pier Herrera

Cristina's Restaurant | Cristina Ceccatelli Cook

Feast Catering | Duane Runswick

Judith McQueen Entertaining | Judith McQueen

Ketchum Grill | Scott Mason and Anne Mason

SEGO Restaurant & Bar | Taite Pearson and Sarah Lipton

Zōu 75 | Sky Barker and Derek Holliday

Wine Consultant

Professional Wine Services

Style Tips Contributors

Bellissimo

Botanica

Sue Bridgman Florist

The Picket Fence

Rasberrys Catering

Taylor'd Events

Style Tips Photographer

Kevin Syms

Event Photography

Dev Khalsa

Hillary Maybery

Paulette Phlipot

Prosciutto Cones

table of contents

introduction

Frequently recognized as one of the "Top Ten" charity wine auctions in the country by *Wine Spectator*, the Sun Valley Center Wine Auction is a three-day celebration of premier wines and delectable food, all for the purpose of raising money for the arts. Now in its 30th year, the Wine Auction has raised over $18 million.

The event features exclusive vintner dinners hosted in private homes with superb locally and nationally recognized chefs, a glamorous Auction Gala, an outdoor concert and picnic, wine tasting and educational symposia. Wine connoisseurs, vintners and generous arts patrons come together to make this event one of the highlights of summer in Sun Valley, Idaho.

For the first time in 30 years, we invite you behind the scenes for a glimpse of this luxurious and festive community event. We will share some of the secrets of its success and give you sumptuous recipes, tips and tools to host memorable parties of your own.

Proceeds from the sale of this book benefit the Sun Valley Center for the Arts educational programs.

Salut!

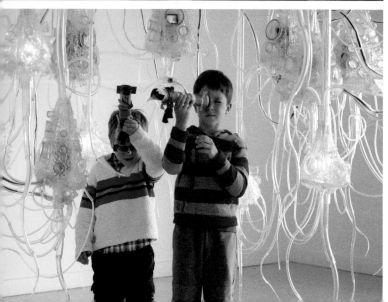

SUN VALLEY CENTER
FOR THE ARTS

the center

Founded in 1971, the Sun Valley Center for the Arts is the oldest arts organization in the Wood River Valley. It was the brainchild of the owner of the Sun Valley Company at the time, Bill Janss, who believed this resort town would never be a whole community without a vibrant arts and cultural life. He enlisted Glenn Cooper, who would later become his wife, to make this dream a reality.

Since then, The Center has grown into a year-round organization that serves up to 37,000 people through exhibitions, performances, lectures and classes. 35% of the participants are children and 90% of the children's programs are free of charge. In 2006 The Center received accreditation from the American Association of Museums and is one of only five AAM accredited institutions in Idaho.

The Center is a primary partner for the Blaine County School District —reaching thousands of children every year with visiting performers, artists and lecturers as well as after-school art classes and guided field trips in our gallery. 100% of these school programs are provided free of charge.

In addition, The Center offers endless adult and family classes, exhibitions and lectures. With its incredible outreach and world-class programming, from visual arts exhibitions by Georgia O'Keeffe, Walton Ford and Alfred Steiglitz to performances by Lyle Lovett, The Vienna Boys Choir and Bonnie Raitt, to lectures by Ira Glass, Sir Salman Rushdie and Terry Tempest Williams, The Center is undoubtedly one of the cornerstones of the Wood River Valley. A defining strength of The Center is how it explores topics of relevance to our times and of interest to our community through in-depth collaboration among the program departments.

The Center also helps students and teachers who want to develop their artistic talents through specialized study by awarding approximately 35 scholarships per year in amounts ranging from $500 to $5,000.

In 2009 a new group emerged from The Center called the Junior Patrons Circle. The JPC is a young(ish) group dedicated to developing the next generation of arts patrons and participants. This book was put together by the Junior Patrons Circle to benefit The Center's educational programming.

The Center appreciates all of its members, donors, wine auction participants, and program attendees for their generous support. If you are not already part of The Center family, we invite you to join us at any of the great events we host throughout the year. We welcome you to become a part of The Center's amazing legacy of providing world-class arts and cultural experiences to residents and visitors of our unique mountain community.

wine tasting party

Take your guests on a flavor adventure by preparing an assortment of appetizers and hors d'oeuvres and serving them with a variety of wines selected to pair with each delicious bite.

wine tasting party

fruit and vegetables | 17

Asparagus Wrapped with Crispy Prosciutto
Bruschetta of Strawberries and Tomatoes with Agreste
Goat Cheese with Cassis Onions
Stuffed Baby Red Potatoes with Crème Fraîche and Caviar
Local Heirloom Melon with Duck Prosciutto, Mint and Saba
Summer Soups: Roasted Butternut Squash Soup and Minted Pea Soup

seafood | 29

Coconut Shrimp with Caribbean Rum Sauce
Crispy Kani Delight Sushi Cakes with Sriracha Aioli
Martini Tartare with Soy Ginger Vinaigrette and Crispy Wonton Chips
Pistachio Encrusted Sea Scallops with Panko Encrusted Eggplant and Red Bell Pepper Pesto
Scallop Ceviche
Seared Tuna on Crispy Wontons with Ginger Tomato Relish

meat and poultry | 43

Chinese 10-Spice Lava Lake Lamb Ribs with Asian BBQ Sauce
Grilled Chicken Skewers with Peanut Sauce
Prosciutto Cones with Citrus Vinaigrette

Asparagus Wrapped with Crispy Prosciutto

Asparagus Wrapped with Crispy Prosciutto
from Feast Catering
serves 6

1 bunch asparagus spears

10 slices prosciutto

vegetable oil

preparation. Blanch asparagus for 2 minutes in boiling water. Immediately transfer to ice water to cool (this keeps the bright green color and crispness). Cut prosciutto into strips about 1½ inches wide by 4 inches long. Take each asparagus spear, and starting right below the tip, roll prosciutto down the length. Keep the prosciutto taut, careful not to tear it. After rolling, a ½-inch of green should show at the bottom and top.

Heat a small amount of vegetable oil in a sauté pan. Once hot, place wrapped asparagus in pan and fry until prosciutto is crispy and golden, about 1 to 2 minutes per side.

final assembly and plating. Arrange on a platter for an appetizer or serve as a side dish for an entrée.

 Try a lively and vibrant white wine with juicy apple, melon or citrus notes like Ferrari-Carano Fumé Blanc or Adelsheim Vineyards Pinot Gris.

Bruschetta of Strawberries and Tomatoes with Agreste

Bruschetta of Strawberries and Tomatoes with Agreste
from Cristina's Restaurant
serves 4 to 6

2 cups strawberries, quartered

1½ cups sweet cherry tomatoes, quartered

½ cup fresh basil chiffonade

1 tablespoon extra virgin olive oil

3 tablespoons Agreste*

salt and pepper to taste

ciabatta loaf, sliced and grilled

preparation. Makes 3½ cups. Gently toss ingredients together. Serve on grilled slices of ciabatta.

*Agreste is a tart, green grape juice made by pressing the grapes before they ripen. It can be found in specialty stores, see sources on page 234.

 A sparkling Rosé or a young Sangiovese pairs well with the flavors of this bruschetta. Try J Brut Rosé or Pietra Santa Sangiovese.

Goat Cheese with Cassis Onions

Goat Cheese with Cassis Onions
from Cristina's Restaurant
serves 4 to 6

1 large red onion, diced
(about 2½ cups)

1 tablespoon extra virgin
olive oil

salt and pepper to taste

¾ cup crème de cassis

¼ cup red wine vinegar

1 tablespoon granulated sugar

1 (8-ounce) fresh goat
cheese log

pinch of fresh thyme

flatbreads, ciabatta or
focaccia

preparation. Makes about 1 cup. Heat olive oil in a large sauté pan over medium heat, add onions, and sauté with salt and pepper until golden and translucent, about 8 minutes. Add crème de cassis and red wine vinegar and cook until alcohol evaporates and onions are glazed, about 4 minutes. Stir in sugar and cook 1 minute. Remove from heat. Set aside.
Slice goat cheese into ½-inch rounds. Broil for 30 seconds on ungreased baking sheet.

final assembly and plating. Place cheese rounds on serving plate and loosely arrange onions on top. Sprinkle with thyme and serve with flatbreads, ciabatta or focaccia.

 Pair with a Chenin Blanc that has a touch of sweetness or a nice herbal Sauvignon Blanc. Try Honig Vineyard Sauvignon Blanc or Pine Ridge Chenin Blanc/Viognier.

Stuffed Baby Red Potatoes

Local Heirloom Melon with Duck Prosciutto

Stuffed Baby Red Potatoes
with Crème Fraîche and Caviar from CIRO Restaurant & Wine Bar
serves 6

½ cup olive oil

12 small baby red potatoes

1 ounce caviar (any type)

2 tablespoons olive oil

1 sprig dill

salt and pepper to taste

Crème Fraîche
(made a day or more in advance)

1 cup heavy cream

¼ cup buttermilk

crème fraîche. Mix the cream and buttermilk together in a glass jar. Let stand at room temperature for 24 hours or more, until mixture thickens and develops a light tangy flavor. Stir and refrigerate before use (crème fraîche will keep in refrigerator for about 2 weeks). Use approximately 1 cup if substituting store-bought crème fraîche.

preparation. Preheat oven to 375°F.
Cut potatoes in half. Hollow out centers with a small spoon or melon baller. Place in water to avoid discoloration while working. When ready, drain in colander and gently dry.
Toss potatoes in mixing bowl with olive oil, salt and pepper. Roast potatoes until golden brown and lightly cooked through, approximately 25 to 30 minutes.

final assembly and plating. Fill potato skins with crème fraîche. Add small scoops of caviar on top. Garnish with dill and serve.

 Perfect with a classic dry, nutty, yeasty-toasty Champagne such as Schramsberg J Schram or Argyle Extended Tirage Brut.

Local Heirloom Melon with Duck Prosciutto
Mint and Saba from SEGO Restaurant & Bar
serves 4 to 6

2 local melons, cut in half, seeds removed

10-12 thin slices of duck prosciutto*

mint, smallest leaves

saba wine syrup*

skewers

preparation. Using a melon baller, cut as many perfect balls from the melons as possible. Thinly slice prosciutto so you have as many slices as you do melon balls. Wrap one slice of prosciutto around each piece of melon. Place a small mint leaf on each ball and skewer through the center of the leaf through one end of the prosciutto, through the melon, and finally through the other end of the prosciutto slice. Ensuring that you put the skewer through both ends of the slice of prosciutto makes sure the duck stays wrapped around the melon ball.

final assembly and plating. Arrange on a platter, drizzle with Saba.

*In lieu of duck prosciutto, prosciutto from pork may be used. Duck prosciutto may be purchased at specialty markets and gourmet delis. Saba is the sweet reduction of grape must. To purchase duck prosciutto or saba, see sources on page 234.

 Look for a medium- to full-bodied white, exuberantly fresh, with tropical fruit and lemon zest. Try Calera Viognier or Duckhorn Sauvignon Blanc.

Roasted Butternut Squash Soup

Minted Pea Soup

Roasted Butternut Squash Soup
from Judith McQueen Entertaining
serves 6 to 8

1 butternut squash, cut in half lengthwise

1 onion, chopped

6 cloves garlic, chopped

2 carrots, chopped

2 leeks, chopped and rinsed (white and light green parts only)

½ cup heavy cream (optional)

2 cups chicken or vegetable stock (enough to cover the squash)

olive oil

salt and pepper to taste

fresh mint (for garnish)

preparation. Preheat oven to 375°F. Brush squash with olive oil and sprinkle with salt and pepper. Roast for 45 minutes or until soft. When cool, remove flesh from the skin.

In a sauce pot, sauté onions, garlic, carrots and leeks until soft, then add roasted squash, stock and heavy cream (if using). Cook for at least 30 minutes. Purée to desired thickness. Soup can be served hot or cool.

final assembly and plating. Garnish with mint leaves. Serve.

Minted Pea Soup
from Judith McQueen Entertaining
serves 4

4 cups low sodium chicken stock (32 ounces)

1 package frozen peas

2 bunches fresh mint

½ cup heavy cream

salt and white pepper to taste

preparation. Bring chicken stock to boil and add peas. Turn heat off and let peas cook for 5 minutes.

Purée peas and stock in blender or food processor (using the chicken stock, bring soup to desired consistency). Put back on stove (while still hot) and add the 2 whole bunches of mint to steep until cool. Put through a strainer to remove the mint. Cool in the refrigerator and then add the cream, salt and white pepper to taste.

final assembly and plating. Garnish with salt and cracked pepper. Serve.

 Try a refreshing, slightly off-dry Riesling or a newly released Pinot Noir Rosé such as Calera Vin Gris of Pinot Noir or Cold Springs Idaho Riesling.

style tips

Brighten your table décor with ribbon votives, spring bulbs and personalized wine charms in a rainbow of colors, texture and style.

floating candles

Tiny votives and floating candles offer elegant and simple centerpiece options. Dress them up and make them look unique by adding a bit of color with decorative ribbon. Ribbon color, texture and pattern options are endless and you can adorn almost any glass or jar with a bit of ribbon and a drop of hot glue. *Courtesy Taylor'd Events.*

spring bulbs

There is nothing like the beauty of flowering spring bulbs. Mix and match all colors and textures (frilly with sleek, smooth with ruffled) for a bright and cheerful mix. Be sure to cut stems on an angle, under running water, to help preserve and ensure a colorful and fresh display. *Courtesy Botanica*.

personalized wine charms

Use stamps in the shape of letters, numbers, animals, bugs or other flora or fauna to create your own design. All you need is a small piece of cardstock, a hole punch, a stamp, ink pad and ribbon. *Courtesy The Picket Fence*.

Coconut Shrimp

Coconut Shrimp
with Caribbean Rum Sauce from CIRO Restaurant & Wine Bar
serves 6

20 large shrimp (15/20 count)

1 cup shredded coconut
(unsweetened)

1 tablespoon Caribbean
jerk spice

1 cup unsalted plain
breadcrumbs

1 cup coconut milk

1 cup all-purpose flour

2 eggs

canola oil

salt and pepper to taste

Caribbean Rum Sauce

1 cup sweet chili sauce

1 lemon, juiced

1 shallot, minced

2 sprigs cilantro

¼ cup rice wine

1 ripe mango,
peeled and pitted

caribbean rum sauce. In a blender, add sweet chili sauce, lemon juice, shallot, cilantro, rice wine and mango. Blend together. Season with salt and freshly ground pepper to taste.

preparation. In a bowl, mix shredded coconut, Caribbean jerk spice and breadcrumbs. Set aside. In separate bowl, whisk coconut milk and eggs together. Place the flour in another bowl.
Grab a shrimp by the tail and dip in the following sequence: flour, egg mixture, breadcrumbs. Repeat for each shrimp and set aside.
Deep fry shrimp in canola oil at 340°F (or medium-high) until light brown and crispy.

final assembly and plating. Place ramekin with rum sauce in middle of plate for dipping and surround with coconut shrimp. Serve immediately.

 Pair with a California Pinot Blanc or a full, rich-styled Viognier. Try Chalone Estate Pinot Blanc or Pride Mountain Vineyards Viognier.

Crispy Kani Delight Sushi Cakes

Crispy Kani Delight Sushi Cakes
with Sriracha Aioli from Zōu 75
serves 6 to 8

½ pound quality crab meat (preferably legs), cooked

½ pound sushi-grade ahi tuna, thinly sliced along the grain

1 cup sushi rice

1¼ cups water

pinch of salt

¾ cup panko breadcrumbs

¾ cup tempura batter, mixed with water

vegetable oil

½ avocado, thinly sliced

½ cup prepared sweet Asian chili sauce

½ red bell pepper, finely chopped

Sriracha Aioli

1 package (17 ounces) Japanese mayonnaise (preferably Kewpie)*

Sriracha (Asian chili sauce) to taste

1 tablespoon soy sauce

sriracha aioli. Blend the Japanese mayonnaise, Sriracha sauce and soy sauce in a mixing bowl to taste. To up the spiciness, add more Sriracha. Set aside.

preparation. Run cold water over rice and rinse several times until water runs clear. Be sure to use Japanese short-grained white (japonica or sushi) rice. Drain the rice, and place in a sauce pot with water and salt. Over high heat, bring to boil for 1 minute while stirring. Cover immediately, turn heat to low and cook rice for 10 to 15 minutes or until water is nearly gone. Turn heat off but keep lid in place and let steam for 10 minutes more.

Mix the cooked rice, crab meat, panko breadcrumbs and prepared tempura batter ingredients in medium bowl. Form mixture into cakes approximately ½-inch thick by 1 inches wide by 3 inches long. Place on wax paper.

Heat vegetable oil (about 1 inch deep) in medium sauté pan. Carefully place cakes in pan, and fry until golden brown. Pat dry with paper towel.

final assembly and plating. Lay the ahi tuna and avocado at an angle over the sushi crab cakes, avocado first. Cut into 1-inch long pieces and separate into a desired pattern. Drizzle the sweet Asian chili sauce over the pieces. Then drizzle with Sriracha aioli. Sprinkle red bell pepper over the top. Serve immediately, accompanied with wasabi, ginger and soy sauce.

*Japanese mayonnaise is made with sesame oil, rather than olive oil. It can be found in Asian specialty stores, see sources on page 234.

Try a light and elegant white with great fruit and balanced acidity such as Chateau Ste. Michelle, Dr. Loosen Eroica Riesling or L'Ecole No. 41 Sémillon.

Martini Tartare

Martini Tartare
with Soy Ginger Vinaigrette and Crispy Wonton Chips from Zōu 75
serves 6

5 ounces sushi-grade ahi tuna, cubed

½ cup English cucumber, cubed

½ cup jicama, cubed

½ avocado, cubed

1 tablespoon green onion, minced

12 wonton skins (approximately 5 inches in diameter)

black sesame seeds (optional)

vegetable oil

Soy Ginger Vinaigrette

½ cup vegetable oil

½ cup sesame oil

¼ cup soy sauce

3 tablespoons Mirin*

3 tablespoons rice vinegar

2 tablespoons yellow onion, minced

1 teaspoon fresh ginger, grated

1 clove garlic, minced

soy ginger vinaigrette. Blend all ingredients for soy ginger vinaigrette in a blender until mixture becomes smooth and consistent. Taste, and adjust flavors as desired. Yields extra dressing that can be stored in refrigerator and used as a marinade or salad dressing.

preparation. Combine cubed ahi tuna, cucumber, jicama, avocado and ¾ of the green onion (reserve remainder for garnish) in a bowl. Lightly coat the tuna mixture with the soy ginger vinaigrette to taste. Set aside for final plating.

crispy wonton chips. Heat 3 to 4 tablespoons vegetable oil in a medium sauté pan on medium-high heat. One at a time, place wonton chips in oil and fry until slightly golden. Dry chips on a paper towel.

final assembly and plating. Place equal portions of the tuna mixture into 6 martini glasses and add chips to each. Garnish with sliced green onion and black sesame seeds or tobiko (optional). For a healthier version, replace fried wonton chips with slices of English cucumber.

NOTE: You will need 6 martini glasses.

*Mirin is a sweet rice wine available at Asian specialty markets, see sources on page 234.

 Pair with rich and spicy white wines with a tropical fruit profile like Au Bon Climat, Clendenen Family Vineyards Tocai or Sleight of Hand Gewurztraminer.

Pistachio Encrusted Sea Scallops

Pistachio Encrusted Sea Scallops
with Panko Encrusted Eggplant and Red Bell Pepper Pesto from Zōu 75
serves 6

6 giant sea scallops,
washed, trimmed and dried

1 cup pistachios

¼ cup flour

salt and pepper to taste

3 eggs, whipped

6 slices French baguette,
sliced ½-inch thick

2 tablespoons olive oil

Red Bell Pepper Pesto

2 to 3 roasted red bell
peppers (fresh or canned)

1 cup fresh basil (reserve a
few leaves for garnish)

½ cup parmesan cheese,
shredded

4 garlic cloves

¼ cup pine nuts

½ cup olive oil

salt and pepper to taste

Panko Encrusted Eggplant

1 Japanese eggplant,
cut into ¾-inch slices

¼ cup flour

3 eggs, whipped

1 cup panko breadcrumbs

2-3 tablespoons olive oil

red bell pepper pesto. Blend the roasted red bell peppers, basil (reserve some for garnish), parmesan cheese, garlic cloves, pine nuts and olive oil in a blender until the sauce is desired consistency. Add salt and pepper to taste. Pour into a small saucepan and heat gently on low.

panko encrusted eggplant. Place flour, egg wash, and panko breadcrumbs side by side in separate shallow bowls. Dip eggplant slices in flour, then in egg wash, then in panko breadcrumbs. Heat olive oil in sauté pan and sear the eggplant on both sides until golden brown. Set aside for final plating.

preparation. Coarsely grind pistachios, flour, salt and pepper in a coffee or spice grinder. Place pistachio mix in a shallow bowl.
Add small amount of water to the egg mix. Coat scallops in egg wash, then coat in pistachio mix.
Heat 2 tablespoons olive oil in medium sauté pan. Brown scallops on both sides and cook to medium rare. The centers should still be slightly translucent (check this by viewing from the side). Remove from the pan. They will continue to cook after you take them off the heat and should still be springy when you press them with your thumb. Set aside for final plating.

final assembly and plating. Lightly grill baguette slices and place on platter. Place scallops on top of eggplant slices. Top with dollops of the red bell pepper pesto and garnish with reserved basil leaves if desired. Serve immediately.

Pair with full-bodied and complex Rhône whites with hazelnut and stone fruit nuances. Try Qupé Marsanne Bien Nacido or Alban Vineyards Rousanne.

Scallop Ceviche

Scallop Ceviche
from CIRO Restaurant & Wine Bar
serves 8

1 pound fresh sushi-grade scallops

1 orange

1 lemon

3 limes

¼ cup green onions, chopped

2 tablespoons cilantro, chopped

1 ounce caviar

salted crackers, deep-fried wontons, sliced cucumbers or tortilla chips

salt and pepper to taste

preparation. Finely dice scallops. Set aside.

Zest orange, lemon and one lime with microplane into small mixing bowl (being careful not to zest down into the rind, as this will impart a bitter flavor). Add juice squeezed from all three limes. Mix in green onions and cilantro. Add scallops and caviar to mixing bowl, and coat with juice mixture. Add salt and pepper to taste, and set aside for 10 minutes before serving.

final assembly and plating. Serve over salted crackers, deep-fried wontons, sliced cucumbers or tortilla chips.

 Try a young, fresh white or a dry Rosé with bright fruit such as Luna Pinot Grigio or Cinder Dry Syrah Rosé.

Seared Tuna on Crispy Wontons

Seared Tuna on Crispy Wontons
with Ginger Tomato Relish from CIRO Restaurant & Wine Bar
serves 6

6 ounces sushi-grade ahi tuna

8-10 wonton skins

2-3 cups vegetable oil

1 tablespoon black sesame seeds

1 tablespoon white sesame seeds

salt and pepper to taste

Ginger Tomato Relish

4 ripe tomatoes

1 shallot, diced

½ teaspoon fresh ginger, grated

1 teaspoon cilantro

1 jalapeno pepper, seeds removed and diced

½ lime, juiced

pinch of black and white sesame seeds

salt and pepper to taste

ginger tomato relish. Prepare the ginger tomato relish in advance to allow flavors to meld. Quarter the tomatoes, and carefully remove seeds and half of the flesh. Dice tomatoes. Place tomatoes, shallots and jalapeno in small mixing bowl. Use a microplane or small grater to zest the fresh ginger. Mix in ginger, cilantro and lime juice. Add sesame seeds, salt and pepper to taste. Set aside.

preparation. Heat about 2 cups vegetable oil to 340°F in a small saucepan. Cut wonton skins in half diagonally to make triangles. Deep fry until golden brown. Set to dry on paper towels.

Heat cast iron or sauté pan until very hot. Encrust tuna with sesame seeds, salt and pepper. When pan starts smoking, add cooking oil. Flash sear tuna for 1 minute on each side. Remove from heat and slice into thin ⅛-inch pieces.

final assembly and plating. Place fried wonton skins on a plate. Add a slice of tuna on top. Garnish with tomato relish. Serve immediately.

 This dish can handle red or white with a big California Chardonnay or Pinot Noir. Try Barnett Sangiacomo Chardonnay or Duckhorn Goldeneye Pinot Noir.

style tips

Create a simple and elegant dessert display to impress your guests and complete your meal.

sweet treats

Create a simple dessert platter for chocolate lovers that is quick and easy. Purchase a selection of hand-dipped or dusted truffles and chocolate covered cookies or macaroons to scatter across a river of caramel sauce. Bamboo skewers with rich brownie slices and raspberry marshmallows add style and flair. *Courtesy Pastry Chef Derek Poirier, Valrhona USA.*

hand-dipped cones

The mini cones can be made from store-bought waffle/sugar cones. Score them with a knife at the desired height and gently break off the top. Dip them in your favorite chocolate and coatings and fill them with your choice of ice cream or sorbet.
Courtesy Rasberrys Catering.

dessert buffet

Offer a different twist for the sweet tooth by providing guests with a beautiful and colorful dessert or candy buffet. Collect a mixture of jars, containers, platters and plates of different sizes and shapes and fill them with colorful treats.
Courtesy Bellissimo.

Chinese 10-Spice Lava Lake Lamb Ribs

Chinese 10-Spice Lava Lake Lamb Ribs
with Asian BBQ Sauce from CK's Real Food
serves 6

5 pounds Lava Lake Lamb* ribs, trimmed of excess fat

Chinese 10-Spice Rub
(can substitute Cajun-style rub)

8 star anise

2 tablespoons fennel seed

2 tablespoons Szechwan peppercorns

1 tablespoon coriander seeds

1½ teaspoons whole black peppercorns

¾ teaspoon whole cloves

¾ teaspoon whole cumin seeds

½ teaspoon ground turmeric

½ teaspoon ground cinnamon

¼ teaspoon ground ginger

salt and pepper to taste

Asian BBQ Sauce

1 quart sweet chili sauce

1 cup soy sauce

½ cup Sriracha (Asian chili sauce)

⅓ cup rice vinegar

¼ cup finely chopped garlic

½ to 1 lime, juiced

salt and pepper to taste

chinese 10-spice rub. Combine all the ingredients for the Chinese 10-spice rub in a spice mill, food processor, or coffee grinder and blend until well combined. This very versatile concoction is great on all types of meat. If chilled, it keeps well for several weeks.

advance preparation. (NOTE: This roasting/steaming part of the process can be done a couple of days ahead.) Preheat oven to 350°F.
Season the ribs generously on both sides with Chinese 10-spice rub. Lay the ribs partially overlapping in one layer in a shallow casserole pan. Add a little water to barely cover the bottom of the dish. Cover tightly with a double layer of aluminum foil. Roast/steam the ribs for 2 hours and 15 minutes in the oven. The rib meat should be tender and barely hanging on the bones.

asian bbq sauce. Place all the ingredients for the Asian BBQ sauce in a bowl and mix together. Taste, adjusting the sweetness to your liking with lime juice. Sauce keeps for several weeks in a jar in the refrigerator.

preparation. Cut the ribs into individual single bone sections. Line a sheet pan with foil, and heat the oven to 400°F. Dip or brush the ribs with Asian BBQ sauce, lay them on the sheet pan, and bake for 20 minutes to heat through. If the ribs are shedding the sauce, give them a little brush touch-up of sauce and a few more minutes in the oven. The ribs should caramelize and the sauce should be sticky.

final assembly and plating. Arrange the ribs on a serving platter. Sprinkle with sesame seeds and thin-sliced scallions or garlic chives. Serve.

*To purchase Lava Lake Lamb ribs, see sources on page 234.

Pull out all the stops with a full flavored rich red such as Paoletti Malbec or KitFox Vineyards Foxy Red, an opulent red blend with generous fruit, round tannins and a sumptuous finish.

Grilled Chicken Skewers

Grilled Chicken Skewers
with Peanut Sauce from CIRO Restaurant & Wine Bar
serves 8 to 10

2 pounds boneless, skinless chicken breasts

1 tablespoon olive oil

1 tablespoon sesame oil

1 tablespoon soy sauce

1 tablespoon sesame seeds

approximately 20 bamboo skewers, soaked in water

Peanut Sauce

½ cup peanut butter

1 can (13 ounces) coconut milk

1 tablespoon olive oil

2 stalks lemongrass, minced

1 celery stalk, minced

3 shallots, minced

4 garlic cloves, minced

2 bay leaves

6 peppercorns

1½ cups white wine

advance preparation. Combine olive oil, sesame oil, soy sauce and sesame seeds in a medium mixing bowl. Slice the chicken breasts lengthwise into 1½- to 2-ounce thin strips. Marinate chicken in mixture for up to 1 hour while preparing the peanut sauce.

peanut sauce. Add olive oil, lemongrass, celery, shallots and minced garlic into a small saucepan and cook on medium-low heat for 5 minutes. Add bay leaf, peppercorns and white wine. Simmer until reduced by half. Add coconut milk and peanut butter. Cook for 10 minutes. Remove from heat and run through a strainer, pressing the sauce out of the vegetables.

preparation. Skewer the chicken lengthwise with bamboo skewers. Place on grill over medium-high heat for 3 to 4 minutes on each side until cooked through but still juicy.

final assembly and plating. Serve on a platter with peanut sauce in a separate bowl for dipping.

 Pair with a French-style Chardonnay or Pinot Noir such as Kistler Vineyard Les Noisetiers Chardonnay or Melville Estate Pinot Noir.

Prosciutto Cones

Prosciutto Cones
with Citrus Vinaigrette from Cristina's Restaurant
serves 6

6 thin slices prosciutto

4 ounces watercress

4 ounces pecorino toscano,*
cut into matchsticks

freshly ground black pepper

Citrus Vinaigrette

6 chive stems, minced

1 teaspoon crushed mustard
seeds

½ lemon, juiced

½ cup extra virgin olive oil

pinch of salt

preparation. Place prosciutto slices on cutting board. Arrange watercress and cheese matchsticks on top, and roll prosciutto into the shape of a cone so the watercress and cheese stick out the top.

citrus vinaigrette. Whisk together chives, mustard seeds and lemon juice in a small mixing bowl. Slowly add olive oil and whisk until mixture reaches a creamy consistency. Whisk in salt and adjust to taste.

final assembly and plating. Lightly coat a serving plate with citrus vinaigrette. Arrange prosciutto cones seam side down on top. Drizzle with a little more citrus vinaigrette, add freshly ground pepper and serve.

*Pecorino Toscano is an Italian cheese available in specialty markets and delis, see sources on page 234.

Try a country Italian Barbera or a barrel-aged Sauvignon Blanc like Merry Edwards Sauvignon Blanc or Renwood Winery Barbera.

outdoor dining

Bring family and friends together under the brilliant summer skies. Enjoy tasteful and stylish dining outdoors with the following menus crafted by some of Sun Valley's finest chefs, all expertly paired with wines to complement each festive dish.

outdoor dining

Menu One | 52

Red Curry Grilled Shrimp with Sweet and Spicy Dipping Sauce
Belgian Endive Salad with Roasted Beets, Crumbled Blue Cheese and Candied Pecans
Rack of Lava Lake Lamb with Rosemary Aioli
Smoked Trout and Jicama Coleslaw
Rebecca's Chocolate Chunk Brownies

Menu Two | 64

Grilled Pizza with Pears, Pecorino and Walnuts
Charred Multicolor Heirloom Tomatoes with Oregano and Thyme
Strange But Good Potatoes
Butterflied Leg of Lamb with Caramelized Lemon Sauce
Limoncello Gelato

Menu Three | 74

Mâche Salad with Garlic Croutons and Bacon Vinaigrette
Pan Seared Halibut with Garlic Creamed Leeks and Potato Confetti
Berries with Crème Anglaise

Menu Four | 84

Bacon Wrapped Scallops with Citrus Gremolata
Mesquite Grilled Idaho Trout with Herbed Butter and Curried Corn Salad
Trio of Pot de Crème

Menu Five | 92

Seafood Gazpacho with Oregon Bay Shrimp, Prawns and Tilapia
Organic Mixed Greens with Dijon Mustard Vinaigrette
Flat Iron Steak with Cilantro Lemon Chimichurri and Pepper Medley
Grilled Stonefruit and Pineapple with Simple Syrup

Menu Six | 104

Sweet Potato Frittatas with Herb Cream
Radicchio Leaves with Apricot Vinaigrette
Mushroom Dust Encrusted Elk Tenderloin with Red Wine and Roasted Shallot Sauce
Chocolate Martini with Chocolate Ganache Rim

Menu Seven | 114

Prosciutto Summer Rolls with Tart Apple Slaw
Turkish Lamb Kebab with Turkish Style Pide and Tomato Peach Chutney
Bing Cherry and Zinfandel Compote with Anne's Lemon Ice Cream

Known for his inspired use of local, seasonal ingredients, Chris Kastner has put together a selection of recipes perfect for a festive candlelit dinner on the terrace or even a gourmet picnic on the lawn.

Menu One

Chef Chris Kastner of CK's Real Food

starter
Red Curry Grilled Shrimp
with Sweet and Spicy Dipping Sauce

Thurston-Wolfe Pinot Gris/Viognier (PGV)

salad
Belgian Endive Salad with Roasted Beets,
Crumbled Blue Cheese and Candied Pecans

Robert Sinskey Abraxas

main
Rack of Lava Lake Lamb
with Rosemary Aioli

Ross Andrew Boushey Vineyard Syrah

side
Smoked Trout and Jicama Coleslaw

Ste. Chapelle Special Harvest Riesling

dessert
Rebecca's Chocolate Chunk Brownies

Quady Elysium Black Muscat

Red Curry Grilled Shrimp

Red Curry Grilled Shrimp
with Sweet and Spicy Dipping Sauce
serves 6

24 jumbo shrimp, peeled
and deveined

2 tablespoons Thai red
curry paste

1 tablespoon canola oil

12 bamboo skewers,
soaked in water

Sweet and Spicy Dipping Sauce

1 cup sweet chili sauce

1 tablespoon lemongrass,
thinly sliced

1 small serrano chili pepper,
minced

1 lime, zested

½ cup lime juice
(about 3 to 5 limes)

2 teaspoons fish sauce

⅓ cup rice vinegar

advance preparation. Peel and devein the shrimp and place in a bowl until ready to use.
Whisk together red curry paste and canola oil in small mixing bowl.
Double skewer shrimp through heads and tails with four shrimp per skewer arranged in a tight compact unit. Continue until all are double skewered. Lay arrangement on sheet pan.
Brush the shrimp generously with the curry paste and canola oil marinade and set aside. This can be done the day before.

preparation. Preheat grill to 400°F. Remove shrimp from the refrigerator, then grill over medium heat for 5 to 7 minutes total, turning once.

sweet and spicy dipping sauce. Use a microplane to zest the lime. Combine the lime zest with the sweet chili sauce, sliced lemongrass, serrano chili pepper, lime juice, fish sauce, and rice vinegar in a blender. Store sauce in a glass jar or other container until ready to serve. Refrigerate. This sauce keeps for a month.

final assembly and plating. Serve with sweet and spicy dipping sauce.

Thurston-Wolfe Pinot Gris/Viognier
(PGV): A crisp, lively white from
Washington with tropical fruit notes.

Belgian Endive Salad with Roasted Beets

Belgian Endive Salad with Roasted Beets,
Crumbled Blue Cheese and Candied Pecans
serves 6 to 8

16 hearts of Belgian endive
(can substitute romaine or
butter lettuce)

1 cup Honey Crisp apple,
sliced

½ cup Rogue Creamery*
blue cheese, crumbled

⅓ cup white balsamic vinegar

¼ cup verjus*

½ cup canola oil

½ tablespoon shallot, minced

salt and pepper to taste

sugar to taste

Roasted Beets

6 young golden beets
(about 2 inches in diameter)

1 tablespoon canola oil

salt and pepper to taste

Candied Pecans

2 cups water

½ cup pecan halves

1 tablespoon sugar

½ tablespoon water

advance preparation. Make beets, balsamic vinaigrette, and candied pecans in advance (all can be prepared a day or two ahead).

roasted beets. Preheat oven to 375°F. Wash and trim stems and roots from beets. Lay the still-wet beets on a triple-layered sheet of aluminum foil. Season beets with salt and pepper, drizzle with oil and roll around to coat. Seal the foil packet so that the beet juice does not leak. Place foil packet on sheet pan and put in oven. Bake for 35 minutes or until tender. Allow beets to cool enough to handle, then rub off skin. Beets will keep for a few days in a plastic zip bag in the fridge.

candied pecans. Bring 2 cups water to boil in small saucepan. Pour in pecan halves and boil for 5 minutes. Drain in colander, discarding water. Put the warm nuts back in the saucepan with sugar and ½ tablespoon water. Cook over medium heat, stirring constantly until sugar melts and water evaporates. Spread pecans on lightly oiled or sprayed sheet pan and bake in middle of oven at 275°F for 30 minutes. Check every 5 minutes and stir until glossy and toasted. The pecans keep for weeks in the freezer, and this process works for other nuts as well.

preparation. Wash and dry the endive, and trim ¼-inch from the firm heart. Set aside. (If Belgian endive is not available, substitute another fresh, firm lettuce leaf that can be used as a scoop or spoon to hold the beet and apple part of the salad.) Combine vinegar, verjus, and shallots in a small mixing bowl. Let marinate for 15 minutes, then whisk in oil and seasoning. Transfer to glass jar or other container until ready to dress the salad (may yield extra dressing). Refrigerate.
Slice 1½ cups of the roasted beets (or chop them into cubes) and mix together with sliced (or cubed) apples. Dress beet and apple mixture with balsamic vinaigrette, careful not to overdo and overdress. Dress salad just before serving because as the salad rests, the acids pull liquid from the ingredients and make it soggy. Add salt and pepper to taste. If desired, add chopped parsley or chives to brighten the flavor.

final assembly and plating. Before serving, mix in blue cheese and ½ cup of the candied pecans. Spoon the beet apple salad onto the lettuce leaves, or platter the mixture and surround by leaves.

*Verjus is a "green juice," typically made from the juice of green grapes, that dates back to medieval Europe. The juice is used in place of vinegar or lemon to add acidity to soups, sauces and dressings and imparts a slightly "sour" taste that does not compete with wine. To purchase verjus or Rogue Creamery cheese, see sources on page 234.

Robert Sinskey Abraxas: A vibrant white blend from Los Carneros that has contrasting weight and concentration.

Rack of Lava Lake Lamb

Rack of Lava Lake Lamb
with Rosemary Aioli
serves 6

3 Lava Lake Lamb* racks (20 ounces each), frenched

2 tablespoons fresh rosemary, chopped

2 tablespoons fresh parsley, chopped

2 tablespoons garlic, minced

4 tablespoons olive oil

salt and pepper to taste

Rosemary Aioli

5 small cloves of garlic, smashed

1 tablespoon fresh rosemary, minced

1 teaspoon rosemary oil*

½ lemon, zested and juiced

2 tablespoons white wine vinegar

1 tablespoon very hot water to adjust viscosity

1 egg yolk (or 1 ounce pasteurized egg yolk)

1 tablespoon Dijon mustard

salt and cayenne pepper, to taste

1 cup canola oil

½ cup olive oil

preparation. The lamb should be cooked the day before you plan to serve it. Preheat oven to 400°F. Preheat grill to 400°F. This makes an elegant picnic first course, and can be made a day ahead. Try and get medium to small-sized frenched racks of lamb, no more than 20 ounces each, that are ready to cook. (If the racks are much bigger, the individual single-bone chops will be too big to eat in one or two bites. Also the cooking time will need to increase by a few minutes.) The fat cap should be trimmed and the bones trimmed in between them.

If you have a mortar and pestle, combine chopped rosemary, parsley, garlic, olive oil, and salt and pepper, and mash for a minute or two to form a nice aromatic herb paste. If not, combine all in a food processor to form a paste. Rub this paste all over the lamb racks and let them rest for a couple of hours.

Grill the lamb on the meaty side over medium-high heat to mark it nicely, about 5 minutes or so. Then put the lamb on a sheet pan and finish roasting in the 400°F oven for 17 minutes until medium rare. Let cool.

rosemary aioli. Zest half the lemon, then juice half. Combine all ingredients in the food processor except the oil. Run for 10 seconds, then drizzle the oil into the food processor in about 20-second intervals (if too fast, the mixture will not emulsify, if too slow it will emulsify and separate as well). The final result should be a thin sauce, not thick like commercial mayonnaise. If it's too thick, thin with water. If it's too thin, add a little more oil. Adjust the seasonings as needed. Alternatively, delete the eggs, canola oil, and olive oil and replace them with 1½ cups of your favorite mayonnaise. Process in food processor, adjusting the thickness as needed. (Note: This classic garlic mayonnaise is great on everything from artichokes to fish and lamb.)

final assembly and plating. Slice the lamb into single-bone chops and arrange on a platter. With 8 bones on a typical rack, three yield 24 chops. Serve with rosemary aioli. This dish is great served warm or cold.

*To purchase Lava Lake Lamb racks or rosemary oil, see sources on page 234.

 Ross Andrew Boushey Vineyard Syrah: A dense, rich Washington Syrah from the Yakima Valley with penetrating black fruits and spice.

Smoked Trout and Jicama Coleslaw

Smoked Trout and Jicama Coleslaw
serves 6 to 8

3 cups green cabbage, julienned

1 cup red cabbage, julienned

2 cups jicama,
peeled and julienned

1 cup carrot,
peeled and julienned

2 Sun Valley Smoked Trout* filets

1 cup coleslaw dressing
(see recipe below)

cilantro or green onions
(optional)

Coleslaw Dressing

½ cup apple cider vinegar

¾ cup sugar

½ teaspoon celery seeds

pinch of cayenne

½ cup mayonnaise

½ cup sour cream

salt and pepper to taste

preparation. Use a mandoline to julienne the cabbage, jicama, and carrots. Skin the smoked trout fillets and flake into small pieces. Combine vegetables and trout in medium mixing bowl and set aside.

coleslaw dressing. Combine vinegar, sugar, celery seeds, cayenne, salt and pepper in a small saucepan and bring to a brief boil, just until sugar dissolves. Allow syrup to cool. (Syrup can be kept in the fridge for up to a month.) Whisk ½ cup of the syrup with mayonnaise and sour cream in a small mixing bowl. Add salt and pepper to taste.

final assembly and plating. Dress the salad to taste no more than 1 hour before serving. Garnish with cilantro or green onions.

NOTE: This coleslaw is a great starting point for several variations. Leave out the trout and add grapefruit segments, or avocado slices and shrimp. Serve as a side with grilled shrimp or lamb ribs. The base dressing can be modified to make it spicy, or kept subtle and served with pulled pork or as part of a fish sandwich.

*To purchase Sun Valley Smoked Trout, see sources on page 234.

 Ste. Chapelle Special Harvest Riesling: A floral, medium-bodied Riesling with fresh fruit and a little sweetness to offset the spice.

Rebecca's Chocolate Chunk Brownies

Rebecca's Chocolate Chunk Brownies
serves 8 to 10

20 ounces quality, semisweet chocolate (4 ounces cut into small pieces, 16 ounces cut into ¼-inch chunks)

6 ounces unsweetened chocolate, cut into small pieces

8 tablespoons unsalted butter

½ cup flour

¼ cup unsweetened cocoa powder

2 teaspoons baking powder

1 teaspoon salt

6 eggs

2 cups granulated sugar

2 teaspoons vanilla extract

½ cup sour cream

powdered sugar, chocolate sauce and/or ice cream (for garnish)

preparation. These brownies are relatively easy, just have all your ingredients ready to go before you start. Use a good quality chocolate (our favorite is TCHO* out of San Francisco). Preheat oven to 325°F.

Spray non-stick spray on a 12 x 17-inch sheet pan. Lay a piece of parchment paper or silicone non-stick baking mat on top, brush with melted butter, dust with flour and shake off the excess.

Sift together flour, unsweetened cocoa powder, baking powder and salt.

Combine unsweetened chocolate, 4 ounces semisweet chocolate, and butter in a double boiler (or a metal bowl over a pot of simmering water) and heat until melted and smooth.

Place the eggs, sugar, and vanilla extract in an electric mixer and whip on high for 90 seconds until slightly thickened. Then mix in the melted chocolate mixture on medium for 30 seconds. Mix in the dry ingredients for another 30 seconds until just combined. Add in sour cream and mix for another 5 to 10 seconds.

Remove the bowl from the mixer and stir in half of the reserved 16 ounces of chocolate chunks by hand, spread the batter onto the sheet pan and sprinkle the remaining chocolate chunks evenly on top of the batter. The batter will be thick, so work quickly to spread it out before it cools too much.

Bake in the center of the oven at 325°F for 20 to 25 minutes. The batter will rise and begin to fall and crack, indicating they are done. Refrigerate for 15 to 30 minutes until completely cooled.

final plating and assembly. Cut when cooled and sprinkle with powdered sugar or top with your favorite ice cream and chocolate sauce. Serve.

*To purchase TCHO chocolate, see sources on page 234.

Quady Elysium Black Muscat: A lovely late harvest Black Muscat from California with roses on the nose and exotic lychee-like fruit.

Cristina's cuisine never fails to surprise and delight. Impress your guests with a sumptuous summer meal under the stars, featuring flavors right out of the garden. Truly outdoor dining at its best!

Menu Two

Cristina Ceccatelli Cook of Cristina's Restaurant

starter
Grilled Pizza
with Pears, Pecorino and Walnuts

Chappellet Chenin Blanc

salad
Charred Multicolor Heirloom Tomatoes
with Oregano and Thyme

Magito River Trace Sauvignon Blanc

side
Strange But Good Potatoes

Siduri Pinot Noir

main
Butterflied Leg of Lamb
with Caramelized Lemon Sauce

Lindstrom Cabernet Sauvignon

dessert
Limoncello Gelato

Grgich Hills Estate Late Harvest Violetta

Grilled Pizza

Grilled Pizza
with Pears, Pecorino and Walnuts
(Pizza Grigliata con Pere, Pecorino e Noci)
serves 6

8 ounces toscano fresco

1½ ripe pears, thinly sliced

½ cup walnut pieces,
coarsely chopped

extra virgin olive oil

freshly ground black pepper
to taste

Pizza Skins

½ tablespoon dry yeast

2¼ cups warm water

5 cups Italian 00 flour
(or substitute all-purpose flour
or any high-gluten flour)

1 tablespoon salt

½ cup flour for dusting and
rolling skins

pizza skins. Makes 10 (12-inch) skins. Extras can be wrapped in plastic and frozen for later use. In the bowl of a stand-up mixer with a blade attachment, dissolve yeast in warm water. Add flour and salt. Mix until dough clumps together, about 3 minutes. Transfer to a lightly floured surface and knead for about 5 minutes or until dough is soft and elastic. Place in bowl, dust with flour, cover with tea towel and let rest in a draft-free place for at least 1 hour or until doubled in volume. Punch down the dough to its original size, then transfer to a lightly floured surface. Divide the dough into 10 balls, dust with flour, cover with towel and let rest for about 30 minutes. Working with one ball at a time, flatten the dough to form a circle. Using the heel of your hand, and working from the center of the ball outwards, or using a rolling pin, stretch it as much as you can, dusting with flour as you go to form a 12-inch skin.
Partially cook the skins for about 1 minute either on the grill or on a baking sheet or pizza stone in a 550°F oven.

preparation. Thinly slice toscano fresco and arrange atop prepared skins. Cover with a single layer of pear slices, then scatter walnuts over top.
Prepare grill (medium heat). Transfer pizzas to grill or 400°F oven and cook until cheese is soft and crust is lightly browned on the bottom.

final assembly and plating. Transfer pizzas to a wooden board. Sprinkle with freshly ground pepper and drizzle with oil. Cut into wedges and serve.

Chappellet Chenin Blanc: A dry
Chenin Blanc with ripe citrus
and mango in a fuller French
sur lie style.

Charred Multicolor Heirloom Tomatoes

Strange But Good Potatoes

Charred Multicolor Heirloom Tomatoes
with Oregano and Thyme
(Pomidoro Grigliati con Oregano e Timo)
serves 6

3 large, firm multicolor heirloom tomatoes, cored, cut in half horizontally

2 tablespoons fresh oregano leaves

2 tablespoons fresh thyme leaves

extra virgin olive oil

salt and pepper to taste

preparation. Arrange tomatoes, cut side up, on rimmed baking sheet. Sprinkle with 1½ tablespoons each oregano and thyme leaves and a little olive oil. Salt and pepper to taste. Let rest until ready to grill.

Using a spatula, place tomatoes, cut side up, on grill. Grill on medium-high heat until charred, then turn and char the other side.

final assembly and plating. Transfer to serving platter and sprinkle with remaining each oregano and thyme, freshly ground black pepper and a few drops olive oil (if desired). Serve warm.

Magito River Trace Sauvignon Blanc: A snappy, light Sauvignon Blanc with spicy pear, quince and yellow apple.

Strange But Good Potatoes
(Patate Strane ma Buone)
serves 4 to 6

12 small red or white new potatoes

extra virgin olive oil

a few rosemary sprigs

salt and pepper to taste

preparation. In a large soup pot, cover potatoes with cold water and add a pinch of salt. Bring water to boil, then reduce heat and simmer until potatoes are al dente, about 30 minutes. With a slotted spoon, gently transfer potatoes to kitchen towel to dry. When potatoes have cooled, use the kitchen towel as a buffer, and smash with the palm of your hand until they split open and flatten to a thickness of about ½ inch.

Arrange potatoes on a cookie sheet brushed with olive oil. Drizzle potatoes with olive oil then sprinkle with salt, freshly ground black pepper and a few rosemary leaves. Loosely cover with kitchen towel until ready to grill.

Heat griddle on medium low. With a spatula, transfer potatoes to the hot griddle. Using a sprig of rosemary, brush the potatoes with olive oil from the cookie sheet. Turn and repeat until potatoes are crisp and *dorate* (lightly bronzed) on both sides.

final assembly and plating. Transfer to platter, sprinkle with more rosemary leaves and serve.

Siduri Pinot Noir: A medium-bodied, cool climate Pinot Noir, featuring Sonoma herbs, cherry and raspberry fruit.

Butterflied Leg of Lamb

Butterflied Leg of Lamb
with Caramelized Lemon Sauce
(Coscia di Agnello con Limoni Caramellati)
serves 6

1 boneless leg of lamb
(approximately 4 pounds)

4 ounces pancetta, thinly sliced

20 fresh sage leaves, divided

4 cloves garlic, 3 chopped,
1 slivered

1 lemon, zested and juiced

3 tablespoons extra virgin
olive oil

salt and pepper to taste

kitchen string

Caramelized Lemon Sauce

1 large lemon, cut into
⅓ inch-thick slices

⅔ cup extra virgin olive oil

3 shallots, thinly sliced

1 clove garlic, thinly sliced

10 fresh sage leaves

3 tablespoons sugar

⅔ cup dry white wine

⅓ cup lemon vodka

2 cups chicken or
beef stock, warmed

salt and pepper to taste

preparation. On a cutting board, open lamb, boned side up, like a book. Trim sinew and fat on the inside, while leaving all the fat on the outside to keep the lamb moist and juicy while grilling. Pound the meat to a uniform thickness of about 1 inch. (Have your butcher do this, if you like.)

Arrange slices of pancetta and 15 sage leaves on the meat. Evenly sprinkle with the chopped garlic, lemon zest and salt and freshly ground black pepper. Starting at one long side, roll lamb up tightly and tie with kitchen string at 2-inch intervals to hold log shape. Using a small knife, make inch-long incisions, about 5 inches apart, all over the lamb and insert a slice of slivered garlic and a piece of sage leaf in each slit. Sprinkle lamb with salt and pepper.

In a medium bowl, whisk together lemon juice, oil and salt and pepper. Rub mixture over entire log. Cover and let marinate until ready to grill.

caramelized lemon sauce. Can be made one day ahead. Heat grill to medium-high heat. Grill lemon slices and set aside. In a saucepan, sauté shallots in olive oil until translucent, about 5 minutes. Add garlic, sage leaves, and grilled lemons. Stir in sugar and cook a few minutes to caramelize. Add wine and vodka to deglaze the pan, and flambé. Add warm stock and let simmer a few minutes. Adjust for salt and pepper. Cover and chill. Rewarm before serving.

To cook, transfer lamb to a hot grill and sear on all sides. Turn the heat to low and grill, brushing occasionally with the sauce and turning every 10 minutes, until thermometer inserted into thickest part registers 130°F, for medium-rare, about 35 to 40 minutes. Transfer to a cutting board and let rest 5 minutes.

final assembly and plating. Slice, arrange on a warm platter and drizzle with sauce. Serve.

 Lindstrom Cabernet Sauvignon: A red berry essence Napa Cabernet with a touch of sage and tarragon spice from the Stag's Leap district.

Limoncello Gelato

Limoncello Gelato
(Gelato al Limoncello)
serves 4 to 8

2 cups heavy cream

½ cup whole milk

¼ cup buttermilk

¼ cup mascarpone

1 whole vanilla bean

4 coffee beans

1 lemon, zested

2 tablespoons lemon juice

4 large egg yolks

⅓ cup sugar

¼ cup Limoncello
plus additional for serving

preparation. Makes 1 quart. Whisk together first 4 ingredients in a large saucepan. Slice vanilla bean in half lengthwise and scrape out seeds. Add vanilla bean and seeds, coffee beans and lemon zest to saucepan. Cook over medium heat, whisking occasionally, until just before boiling point. Remove from heat, cover, and let infuse about 15 minutes.

In a large bowl, whisk together egg yolks, sugar and lemon juice until pale in color and fluffy, about 3 to 4 minutes. Slowly whisk warm cream mixture into yolk mixture. Return mixture to same saucepan and heat on low, stirring with a wooden spoon until thick enough to coat the back of the spoon, about 8 to 10 minutes. Remove saucepan from heat. Strain mixture into a bowl to remove vanilla bean, vanilla bean seeds and coffee beans. Immediately place the bowl in an ice bath. Stir in Limoncello. When mixture has chilled, process in ice cream maker according to manufacturer's instructions. Transfer to freezer container, cover and freeze for up to 2 days.

final assembly and plating. Scoop and serve drizzled with Limoncello.

NOTE: Recipe requires an ice cream maker. Limoncello is an Italian lemon liqueur.

Grgich Hills Estate Late Harvest
Violetta: Reach for a classic
with this late harvest wine with
balanced richness.

Simple foods combined with a creative flair make for an irresistibly delicious feast. Duane Runswick shares a trio of recipes to tempt any appetite, satisfy any craving and amaze all your guests.

Menu Three

Chef Duane Runswick of Feast Catering

salad
Mâche Salad with Garlic Croutons
and Bacon Vinaigrette

Lemelson Pinot Gris, Tikka's Run

main
Pan Seared Halibut
with Garlic Creamed Leeks and Potato Confetti

Raymond Reserve Chardonnay

dessert
Berries with Crème Anglaise

Duckhorn Vineyards Miel

Mâche Salad

Mâche Salad
with Garlic Croutons and Bacon Vinaigrette
serves 4 to 6

½ pound mâche lettuce

2 bacon slices, cooked,
drained (reserve fat),
then chopped

1 teaspoon bacon drippings

2 tablespoons white
wine vinegar

2 teaspoons Dijon mustard

1 tablespoon parsley

¼ cup olive oil

salt and pepper to taste

Garlic Croutons

small baguette, cut into
1-inch squares

8 tablespoons butter, melted

4 garlic gloves, chopped

1 tablespoon parsley, chopped

salt and pepper to taste

garlic croutons. Preheat oven to 375°F. Melt butter, garlic, parsley, salt and pepper together in small saucepan. Place baguette squares in large plastic zip bag with melted butter mixture and shake until well coated. Pour croutons onto baking sheet. Bake for 15 minutes or until golden brown. Set aside for final plating.

preparation. Wash and dry lettuce. Wisk bacon drippings, vinegar, mustard, parsley, salt and pepper in a small metal mixing bowl. When well blended, slowly add olive oil in a small steady stream while whisking vigorously. Adjust or increase amount of olive oil as desired.

final assembly and plating. Lightly dress mâche greens and pile in the middle of a small plate. Sprinkle chopped bacon over greens. Garnish with garlic croutons. Serve.

 Lemelson Pinot Gris, Tikka's Run:
A slightly fuller Oregon Pinot Gris
from the Willamette Valley with
Bosc pear and a pleasant minerality.

Pan Seared Halibut

Pan Seared Halibut
with Roasted Garlic Creamed Leeks and Potato Confetti
serves 4 to 6

4-6 halibut filets (8 ounces each)

1 garlic bulb, roasted

4 leeks, green stalks removed

2 red potatoes

½ cup chicken stock

1 cup heavy cream

½ bunch parsley, chopped

flour

olive oil

advance preparation. Preheat oven to 350°F. Trim an ⅛-inch slice from the top of garlic bulb to just barely expose cloves inside. Place bulb on baking sheet, and drizzle liberally with olive oil. Roast for 45 to 60 minutes or until garlic is soft and caramelized. Remove from oven. Let cool to room temperature.

Cut leeks in half lengthwise (white parts only). Rinse under cold running water, careful not to let the layers separate or fall apart. Cut the halved leeks lengthwise again in small, thin strips. Reserve in bowl of cold water until ready to cook, then drain and dry.

preparation. Preheat oven to 350°F. Peel and brunoise potatoes (first cut into julienne slices, turn a quarter turn, and dice again, producing small cubes of consistent shape and size). Soak in water to prevent browning until ready to cook. Drain potatoes and towel pat dry. Heat 3 to 4 tablespoons oil in a sauté pan. Lightly coat potatoes in flour. Fry until brown.

Heat 2 to 3 tablespoons oil in an ovenproof sauté pan. Place fish in pan, presentation side down, and sear until golden brown crust forms. Flip fish, then place pan in oven. Cook for 8 to 10 minutes or until fish is firm and starting to flake.

While fish is in oven, heat 4 to 6 tablespoons oil in large sauté pan. Add leeks and cook until shiny and glassy, about 3 to 4 minutes on high heat. Deglaze the pan with chicken stock and simmer for 1 minute. Add heavy cream and 6 to 8 roasted garlic cloves, roughly smashed into a paste. Cook until leeks become soft and sauce thickens.

Finish with chopped parsley and salt to taste. Thin leeks out with additional stock as desired.

final assembly and plating. Place heaping pile of leeks in center of plate. Perch halibut on top. Garnish heavily with potato confetti, chopped parsley, or sautéed vegetable of choice (grilled asparagus, sautéed summer squash, zucchini or other).

Raymond Reserve Chardonnay:
A rich non-malolactic Napa
Valley Chardonnay with a touch
of French oak.

Berries with Crème Anglaise

Berries with Crème Anglaise
serves 4 to 6

1 pint raspberries

1 pint blackberries

1 pint blueberries

mint leaves

Crème Anglaise

1 cup heavy cream

4 egg yolks

⅓ cup sugar

preparation. Clean berries and mix together in a small bowl.

crème anglaise. In a small heavy saucepan, heat cream until bubbles form at edges. While cream is heating, whisk together egg yolks and sugar until smooth. Slowly pour ½ cup of the hot cream into the egg yolks, whisking constantly. Gradually add egg yolk mixture back to remaining cream mixture, stirring constantly. Continue to cook over medium-low heat, stirring constantly, until the mixture coats the back of a wooden spoon.

final assembly and plating. Divide berries into 4 to 6 serving bowls and top with crème anglaise. Garnish with mint leaves. Serve.

Duckhorn Vineyards Miel:
A classic pairing with a Sauternes-style Sémillon/Sauvignon late harvest blend.

style tips

Creative containers and picnic caddies, a wine barrel lid as a platter or silver spoons as individual hors d'oeuvres— add a whimsical touch that your guests will remember.

mediterranean spoons

Repurposed spoons make whimsical and colorful appetizer serving platters. Serve guests bite size portions. Use gourmet spread, chutneys or tapenades in a rainbow of colors.
Courtesy Judith McQueen Entertaining.

pass the cheese, please

A wine barrel top makes a fun and unique serving tray. Available through local wineries or wine distributors, you can even turn it into a spinning tray by adding Lazy Susan bearings, available at most hardware or craft supply stores. *Courtesy Rasberrys Catering.*

colorful carryall

Don't be afraid of color when using reclaimed containers as useful picnic caddies. No assembly required. Use the caddy to set your theme and play off the existing graphics and design…or create your own with a glue stick, ribbon, paper cut-outs or tissue paper. *Courtesy Judith McQueen Entertaining.*

Using the freshest ingredients available, Chef Duane Runswick has created these delectable dishes packed with flavor, ideal for an evening of dining al fresco with good friends and great wine.

Menu Four

Chef Duane Runswick of Feast Catering

starter
Bacon Wrapped Scallops
with Citrus Gremolata

Spottswoode Sauvignon Blanc

main
Mesquite Grilled Idaho Trout
with Herbed Butter and Curried Corn Salad

Marimar Torres La Masia Chardonnay

dessert
Trio of Pot de Crème

Chappellet Moelleux

Bacon Wrapped Scallops

Bacon Wrapped Scallops
with Citrus Gremolata
serves 4 to 6

10 to 12 medium day boat scallops

½ pound thick-style bacon

½ bunch parsley, chopped

1 bunch spinach leaves or other leafy greens

3 tablespoons vegetable oil

toothpicks

Citrus Gremolata

2 lemons, zested

2 limes, zested

2 teaspoons olive oil

salt to taste

preparation. Cook bacon strips until halfway done (they will crisp when cooked on the scallop).

citrus gremolata. Combine zest, parsley, olive oil and salt to taste in a small mixing bowl to make citrus gremolata.

Remove adductor muscle from scallop (if still present). Tightly wrap one bacon strip around each scallop (or half a bacon strip, depending on the size of the scallop). Hold in place with small toothpick.

Heat 3 tablespoons vegetable oil in large sauté pan until almost smoking. Cook each side of scallop for about 2 to 3 minutes, or until golden brown and somewhat firm.

final assembly and plating. Serve each scallop on a bed of greens with a dollop of gremolata.

Spottswoode Sauvignon Blanc: A Graves-style Sauvignon Blanc from the Napa Valley with concentration and a long finish.

Mesquite Grilled Idaho Trout

Mesquite Grilled Idaho Trout
with Herbed Butter and Curried Corn Salad
serves 4

4 Idaho trout filets (6-8 ounces each), skin on

mesquite grilling planks

4 ounces butter, softened

½ bunch parsley, chopped

½ bunch cilantro, chopped

1 lemon, sliced into wedges (optional)

salt and pepper to taste

Curried Corn Salad

4 ears sweet summer corn

2 teaspoons curry powder

1 teaspoon cumin, ground

3 tablespoons olive oil

1 tablespoon parsley, chopped

salt to taste

advance preparation. Soak mesquite planks in water for at least 1 hour prior to grilling. Finely chop parsley and cilantro. Mix well with softened butter. Drop ball of herbed butter onto center of 6 x 9-inch piece of plastic wrap. Fold plastic over butter and form into a small cylindrical tube by twisting ends tight. Refrigerate before use.

curried corn salad. Husk corn and remove silk. Cut off kernels with a sharp knife or mandoline. Mix all ingredients in a bowl. Let sit at room temperature for at least one hour before serving, allowing flavors to meld.

preparation. Heat grill to 400°F. Lay trout on mesquite plank, skin side down. Place on grill and close lid. Cook over medium heat for 7 to 9 minutes without disturbing or flipping fish. Remove plank when done and let cool slightly.

final assembly and plating. Remove fish filet and place on plate. Remove butter cylinder from plastic and slice into coin-sized pats. Place one pat on each filet. Garnish with lemon, salt and pepper to taste. Spoon curried corn salad onto plate and serve with green salad.

Marimar Torres La Masia
Chardonnay: Classic Old World
Chardonnay wrapped around
luscious Russian River Valley fruit.

Trio of Pot de Crème

Trio of Pot de Crème
serves 4

½ cup milk

2 cups cream

5 egg yolks

¼ cup white sugar

pinch of salt

1 ounce bittersweet chocolate

½ pint blackberries, crushed

2 tablespoons white sugar

preparation. Preheat oven to 375°F with rack in center of oven.

Make crème anglaise by scalding the milk and 1½ cups cream, careful not to boil over. In a mixing bowl, whisk egg yolks, sugar, and salt until sugar dissolves. Slowly whisk the milk/cream mixture into the egg yolks, stirring constantly so that the eggs don't cook.

Melt chocolate in double-boiler or metal heatproof bowl over simmering water. Split crème anglaise into 3½-cup ramekins per serving. Combine the first with melted chocolate, the second with crushed blackberries, and leave the third plain. Repeat with the remaining 9 ramekins. Place the filled ramekins in a baking dish. Pour in enough hot water to come up halfway on the ramekins. Cover dish with foil and bake for 30 minutes or until set when lightly shaken. Cool for at least 3 hours in the refrigerator.

final assembly and plating. Before serving, use hand mixer to whip the remaining ½ cup heavy cream while adding 2 tablespoons sugar until soft peaks form. Use whipped cream to garnish the chocolate pot de crème. Serve.

NOTE: You will need 12 ½-cup size ramekins or demitasse cups to prepare this dish.

Chappellet Moelleux:
A caramelized, honeyed, mouth-watering and intense late harvest gem.

Chef Duane Runswick offers a taste of summer with these four recipes, taking the basics and enhancing them with innovative twists. His dishes include an exciting variety of ingredients, presenting a full spectrum of flavor.

Menu Five

Chef Duane Runswick of Feast Catering

starter
Seafood Gazpacho
with Oregon Bay Shrimp, Prawns and Tilapia

Buty Sémillon, Sauvignon and Muscadelle

salad
Organic Mixed Greens
with Dijon Mustard Vinaigrette

Turnbull Sauvignon Blanc

main
Flat Iron Steak with Cilantro Lemon
Chimichurri and Pepper Medley

Ridge Vineyards Cabernet Sauvignon/Merlot

dessert
Grilled Stonefruit and Pineapple
with Simple Syrup

Calera Dessert Viognier

Seafood Gazpacho

Seafood Gazpacho
with Oregon Bay Shrimp, Prawns and Tilapia
serves 4

½ pound wild caught cooked bay shrimp

6 prawns (21/25 count)

1 tilapia filet

1 can (8-ounces) diced tomatoes

1 cup tomato juice

3-4 garlic cloves

2 teaspoons prepared horseradish

½ cup cilantro, chopped

1 tablespoon lemon juice

⅛ teaspoon chili powder

1 red bell pepper, diced

1 green bell pepper, diced

2 tablespoons parsley

1-2 lemons, sliced into wedges

preparation. In a food processor, combine diced tomatoes, tomato juice, garlic, horseradish, cilantro, lemon juice and chili powder. Blend for 15 seconds on highest setting. Stir in diced bell peppers.
Grill or sauté tilapia. Let cool, then break into small chunks. Devein prawns and remove tails. Cook in boiling water for 2 minutes. Promptly cool in an ice bath. When cooled, slice prawns in half lengthwise.

final assembly and plating. In a glass or a shallow bowl, place a few chunks of fish, a few tablespoons of bay shrimp and a few prawn halves. Pour a few tablespoons of sauce over seafood. Garnish with chopped parsley and lemon wedges. Serve.

 Buty Sémillon, Sauvignon and Muscadelle: A classic white Bordeaux-style in three-part harmony from Walla Walla, this dry white pairs well with nearly any seafood.

Organic Mixed Greens

Organic Mixed Greens
with Dijon Mustard Vinaigrette
serves 4 to 6

¼ pound organic mixed greens

1 carrot, peeled and thinly julienned

1 tomato, sliced and quartered

½ cup pomegranate seeds

Dijon Mustard Vinaigrette

2 tablespoons white wine vinegar

2 teaspoons Dijon mustard

1 tablespoon parsley

¼ cup olive oil

salt and pepper to taste

preparation. Wash and dry greens. Set aside. Slice tomato into ¼-inch pieces, then quarter and set aside.

dijon mustard vinaigrette. Whisk vinegar, mustard, parsley, salt and pepper in a small metal mixing bowl. When well blended, slowly add olive oil in a small steady stream while whisking vigorously. Taste. Adjust flavor profiles and add additional oil as desired.

final assembly and plating. Lightly dress salad greens. Divide between 4 to 6 salad plates. Sprinkle carrots and pomegranate seeds on top. Serve.

Turnbull Sauvignon Blanc:
A bright Sauvignon Blanc, with fresh fruit flavors of grapefruit, guava and melon.

Flat Iron Steak

Flat Iron Steak
with Cilantro Chimichurri and Pepper Medley
serves 6

2 flat iron steaks (1 pound each)

1 bunch cilantro, minced

4 garlic gloves, minced

⅛ teaspoon red pepper flakes

⅛ cup lemon juice

2 red peppers, julienned

2 green peppers, julienned

2 yellow peppers, julienned

olive oil

advance preparation. Cut each of the 1-pound flat iron steaks into 3 portions (for a total of 6 portions). In a small mixing bowl, combine cilantro, garlic, red pepper flakes, and lemon juice. Pour half over steaks (reserving half in a bowl for garnish later). Cover the steaks and marinate overnight.

preparation. Preheat grill to 400°F. Remove meat from chimichurri marinade and set aside. Cook meat on 400°F grill to medium rare or preferred temperature. Let rest for a few minutes.
Julienne bell peppers. Heat a small amount of olive oil in a medium-size saucepan, and sauté peppers until soft and shiny.

final assembly and plating. Garnish each steak with one tablespoon of chimichurri and add a small pile of bell peppers medley on the side. Serve with roasted new potatoes or grilled vegetables.

Ridge Vineyards Cabernet Sauvignon/Merlot: A classic Bordeaux blend with crème de cassis and rich blackberry fruit.

Grilled Stonefruit and Pineapple

Grilled Stonefruit and Pineapple
with Simple Syrup
serves 4

2 ripe peaches,
pitted and sliced

2 ripe nectarines,
pitted and sliced

2 ripe donut peaches,
pitted and sliced

1 ripe pineapple,
cored and sliced

1 cup heavy cream

mint leaves (for garnish)

olive oil

Simple Syrup

2 cups cane sugar

2 cups water

simple syrup. Combine sugar and water in saucepan. Bring to a boil to dissolve sugar. Remove from heat to let cool.

preparation. Preheat grill to 450°F. Pit all fruit, then slice peaches and nectarines into ½-inch wedges. Core pineapple and slice into ½-inch thick slices. Whip the cream until soft peaks form and set aside.
Adjust grill to medium heat. Lightly coat all fruit with olive oil, then grill (about 2 minutes on each side). Be careful not to move them around too much as you want clean, defined grill marks on both sides of fruit (this makes the dish beautiful).

final assembly and plating. Cut pineapple into smaller chunks and then in alternating layers make a pile with the fruit in the center of the plate. Brush the fruit with the simple syrup and then add a dollop of unsweetened whipped cream to the top. Garnish with mint sprig. Serve.

Calera Dessert Viognier:
Exotic, tropical, honeysuckle
with candied lemon peel,
peach and pineapple richness.

style tips

Candlelight adds an elegant glow to any table. Make it special by using decorative glasses, a creative container or floral accents.

decorative votive holders

Head to the cabinet and grab decorative juice or highball glasses that are etched, textured or engraved. Drop a votive candle into the glass, display it on a decorative platter or cheeseboard, and you have a unique look that ties perfectly into your dinnerware theme. *Courtesy Bellissimo.*

a bed of roses

A fabulous centerpiece can be made very simply using only a small amount of roses. Gather some small glass vases or bowls to highlight a selection of a few perfect blooms, then scatter rose petals down the table and around mini-votives for a simple and romantic effect. *Courtesy Botanica*.

drink caddy votives

A hand-forged drink caddy can also be a candle centerpiece, dressing up your outdoor dining occasion with candlelight that won't blow out with the first breeze. Highball glasses protect the flame from the elements and clustered together, add a soft glow to any table. *Courtesy Bellissimo*.

Judith McQueen's menus, complete with creative presentation, are always crowd-pleasers. From start to finish, this meal brims with richness and intensity and will have your guests asking for more.

Menu Six

Chef Judith McQueen of Judith McQueen Entertaining

starter
Sweet Potato Frittatas
with Herb Cream

The Hess Collection Bodega Colomé Torrontés

salad
Radicchio Leaves
with Apricot Vinaigrette

Deloach OFS Chardonnay

main
Mushroom Dust Encrusted Elk Tenderloin
with Red Wine and Roasted Shallot Sauce

Forman Cabernet Sauvignon

dessert
Chocolate Martini
with Chocolate Ganache Rim

Sweet Potato Frittatas

Sweet Potato Frittatas
with Herb Cream
serves 12

2 sweet potatoes

2 red peppers

2 yellow peppers

10 eggs

2 tablespoons Dijon mustard

1 whole onion, chopped

1 green zucchini, sliced

1 yellow zucchini, sliced

1 cup grated cheddar cheese

Tabasco to taste

salt and pepper to taste

Herb Cream

2 tablespoons fresh chives, minced

2 tablespoons fresh thyme, minced

2 tablespoons fresh oregano, minced

¾ cup sour cream

advance preparation. Peel and slice sweet potatoes ⅛-inch thick or smaller, using a mandoline if desired. Parboil just until tender and cooked through, but still solid. Strain and place on paper towels to soak up any residual water. Set aside. Roast the peppers at 400°F until blistered. Take out and put into paper bag to steam for about 15 minutes. Peel. Cut into large pieces and set aside.

herb cream. Mince the fresh herbs (chives, thyme and oregano). Add ¼ of the herbs to sour cream. Refrigerate until ready to use.

preparation. Preheat oven to 350°F. Mix eggs with remaining ¾ of the herbs, mustard, Tabasco, salt and pepper.
Sauté chopped onions and sliced zucchini until they start to brown, then remove from heat and add salt and freshly ground pepper to taste.
Spray a casserole dish with cooking spray and place sweet potatoes in a single layer at the bottom. Pour some of the egg mixture over it. Add sautéed zucchini and onions, again in a single layer. Pour on more egg mixture. Finally, add the layer of peeled roasted peppers (you can keep these in large pieces, just try to cover the zucchini evenly). Add the rest of the egg mixture. Sprinkle cheese on top and bake at 350°F until a knife comes out clean. This will take between 40 to 50 minutes depending on the frittata's thickness. Remove from oven and set aside until cool to touch.

final assembly and plating. Cut the frittata into squares, plate and top with a squeeze of herbed sour cream. Serve.

 The Hess Collection Bodega Colomé Torrontés: A floral, spicy white that is the most popular white in Argentina.

Radicchio Leaves

Radicchio Leaves
with Apricot Vinaigrette
serves 6

2 heads radicchio, washed, leaves separated and left whole

¼ cup white balsamic vinegar

½ cup extra virgin olive oil

1 small shallot

1 tablespoon apricot jam

3 tablespoons dried apricots, minced

salt and pepper to taste

preparation. In a food processor or blender, process shallot until minced, add the vinegar and olive oil slowly. Once blended, add the apricot jam, 2 tablespoons minced apricots, salt and freshly ground pepper to taste.

final assembly and plating. Place a leaf on a plate and drizzle a teaspoon or so of the vinaigrette on top and repeat until all leaves are stacked. Sprinkle remaining tablespoon of dried apricots around decoratively as garnish.

 Deloach OFS Chardonnay: An elegant and complex Chardonnay, with velvety mouthfeel and length.

Mushroom Dust Encrusted Elk Tenderloin

Mushroom Dust Encrusted Elk Tenderloin
with Red Wine and Roasted Shallot Sauce
serves 4

1 whole elk tenderloin

1 cup dried mushrooms, ground into dust

olive oil

salt and pepper to taste

Red Wine and Roasted Shallot Sauce

10 shallots, peeled and quartered

2-4 tablespoons olive oil

2 cups of red wine

1 cup beef stock

salt and pepper to taste

advance preparation. Preheat oven to 400°F. Cut the elk into 6-ounce steaks (elk tenderloins vary so you may get more or less out of a piece). Use a food processor or spice mill to grind dried mushrooms into dust. Roll the steaks in mushroom dust. Heat olive oil in a sauté pan, and sear steaks until nice and brown. Salt and pepper them, then set aside.

red wine and roasted shallot sauce. Roast the shallots in 2 to 4 tablespoons of olive oil in the preheated oven (400°F) until well colored and almost caramelized (about 25 to 35 minutes).

preparation. Preheat grill. When the shallots are almost done, combine the wine and stock in a small sauce pot over medium heat and reduce by half. Add ½ of the roasted shallots and reduce to ¾ of a cup (the shallots will help to thicken the sauce). Add the rest of the shallots and cook for a few more minutes. Salt and pepper to taste.
Grill the tenderloins on a medium to hot flame until a nice crust forms and set to the side of the grill until the internal temperature is 120°F. Let rest for 5 minutes.

final assembly and plating. Serve the steak with a tablespoon of the sauce, also delicious with creamy Idaho mashed potatoes and frenched green beans.

 Forman Cabernet Sauvignon: A Napa Valley Mountain Cabernet that is voluptuous, flamboyant, multidimensional and soaring.

Chocolate Martini

Chocolate Martini
with Chocolate Ganache Rim
serves 6 (cocktail recipe is for 1 each, made to order)

1½ ounces chocolate vodka

1 ounce clear chocolate liqueur

1 ounce espresso (instant is fine if you don't have an espresso machine)

1 ounce cold water

Chocolate Ganache

1 cup heavy cream

4 tablespoons sweet butter

3 cups bittersweet chocolate chips

chocolate ganache. Heat the butter and cream until just boiling, pour over the chocolate chips, stir and let stand for about 1 minute. Whisk the cream mixture into the chocolate until a nice, thick sauce is formed with no lumps. This sauce will keep for one month in your refrigerator and can be used for lots of things.

preparation. Dip the rims of the martini glasses in the chocolate ganache and place in freezer.

final assembly and plating. Fill a shaker with ice, then add vodka, chocolate liqueur, espresso and water. Shake, and pour into prepared chocolate-rimmed glass. Serve immediately. Repeat as necessary.

NOTE: You will need 6 martini glasses.

Scott Mason shares some of his unique and inventive creations to produce a mouth-watering meal. The mix of savory and sweet throughout the menu is sure to please every palate.

Menu Seven

Chef Scott Mason of Ketchum Grill

starter
Prosciutto Summer Rolls
with Tart Apple Slaw

Rusack Vineyards Sangiovese

main
Turkish Lamb Kebab with Turkish Style Pide
and Tomato Peach Chutney

Gramercy Cellars Syrah

dessert
Bing Cherry and Zinfandel Compote
with Anne's Lemon Ice Cream

Dolce Late Harvest Dessert Wine

Prosciutto Summer Rolls

Prosciutto Summer Rolls
with Tart Apple Slaw
serves 8

8-10 thin slices of prosciutto

2 tart green or tart red apples, julienned

¼ cup dried zante currants

½ orange, zested

freshly ground black pepper

green herbs, for garnish (optional)

Slaw Dressing

1 egg yolk

¼ cup lemon juice

¼ cup red wine vinegar

¼ cup Dijon mustard

2 cups pomace or pure olive oil

2 tablespoons honey

advance preparation. Prepare the slaw dressing by combining the egg yolk, lemon juice, red wine vinegar, Dijon mustard and olive oil in a quart container. Using an immersion blender, emulsify the dressing by starting at the bottom and pulling the blender slowly upward to emulsify. Add the honey and blend again. This dressing is best if made in advance so the flavors can meld.

preparation. In a bowl combine apple julienne, ½ cup of the prepared slaw dressing, the currants and long ribbons of orange zest from half of the orange. Add two turns of black pepper. Toss lightly to combine, but carefully so as not to break the apples.

final assembly and plating. Assemble the summer rolls. High quality and very thinly sliced prosciutto will make this dish sublime.

Lay out the slices of prosciutto on a work table and divide the slaw between the slices. Place the slaw toward the end closest to you. Start by rolling away from you and roll each slice tightly around the slaw. Place on a serving platter. Garnish with fresh green herbs or a drizzle of balsamic vinegar reduction.

 Rusack Vineyards Sangiovese:
A Tuscan-influenced hillside
Sangiovese, with smooth, balanced,
raspberry/currant fruit.

Turkish Lamb Kebab

Turkish Lamb Kebab
with Turkish Style Pide and Tomato Peach Chutney
serves 6 to 8

2½ pounds ground Lava Lake Lamb*

1½ shallots, diced

¼ cup currants

¼ cup pine nuts, toasted

2 cloves garlic, minced

1½ tablespoons salt

1½ tablespoons ground cinnamon

¾ teaspoon ground clove

¾ teaspoon ground fenugreek*

12 metal or bamboo skewers

1 head bibb lettuce, washed, dried and chopped

1 pint Greek yogurt

Tomato Peach Chutney

3 tomatoes, chopped

½ yellow onion, diced

½ cup fresh peach, pitted and diced

½ lime, diced with rind

¼ orange, diced with rind

½ cup red wine vinegar

1 cup brown sugar

2 tablespoons chili powder

pinch of salt

Turkish Style Pide (Flatbread)

2 cups durum flour

½ tablespoon sea salt

1 cup lukewarm water

1 teaspoon dry yeast

pinch of sugar

advance preparation. To make the Turkish style pide (flatbread), proof the yeast with sugar and water. Combine flour and salt. Mix in yeast mixture. Knead for 10 minutes until smooth. Set aside to rest and rise for 30 to 45 minutes. The dough can be made a day ahead and stored in the refrigerator.

tomato peach chutney. Place the chopped tomatoes, diced onion, peach, lime, and orange with the vinegar, brown sugar, chili powder and salt in a large pot and bring to a boil. Reduce heat and simmer for 25 to 40 minutes. The end product will have some liquid remaining, but should not be runny. Cool and set aside. Meanwhile, mix the lamb, shallots, currants, pine nuts, garlic, salt and spices together in a large mixing bowl. Shape mixture onto skewers in about the size and shape of a hot dog. Grill on BBQ for 15 to 20 minutes.

turkish style pide (flatbread). While lamb is cooking, measure the pide dough into 2- to 3-ounce balls. Knead each ball briefly and allow to rest for 15 minutes. Roll out into rounds or ovals with pin on floured surface. Cook ovals on lightly-oiled griddle on medium heat until light brown on both sides.

final assembly and plating. Top Turkish style pide with lamb kebab, bibb lettuce, tomato chutney and a dollop of Greek yogurt. Serve.

*To purchase Lava Lake Lamb, see sources on page 234. If ground fenugreek is not available, you may substitute ground fennel.

Gramercy Cellars Syrah: A bold and complex Washington Syrah with pepper, licorice, smoke and intensely rich, elegant black fruit.

Bing Cherry and Zinfandel Compote

Bing Cherry and Zinfandel Compote
with Anne's Lemon Ice Cream
serves 8 to 10

2 pounds fresh Bing cherries, washed and pitted

1½ cups red Zinfandel

½ cup clover honey

¼ teaspoon ground cinnamon

1 piece star anise

Anne's Lemon Ice Cream

2 cups heavy cream

2 cups milk

2 cups sugar

4 whole lemons

½ teaspoon vanilla

pinch of salt

anne's lemon ice cream. Whisk together cream, milk and sugar until sugar has dissolved. Finely grate the rind of two of the lemons and add to the cream. Juice all four of the lemons and strain out seeds and pulp. Add to cream, along with salt and vanilla. Process in an ice cream maker according to manufacturer's instructions.

preparation. Place cherries, Zinfandel, honey, cinnamon and anise in a sauce pot and cook together on medium heat until cherries are cooked, about 10 minutes.

final assembly and plating. Serve cherry compote warm over Anne's lemon ice cream (not too hot, or the ice cream will become soupy).

NOTE: Recipe requires ice cream maker.

 Dolce Late Harvest Dessert Wine: The essence of California late harvest wine with rich honeyed-dried apricots.

vintner dinners

Experience the unique style and grace of some past vintner dinners through a sampling of menus created by acclaimed chefs in collaboration with the owners and winemakers of legendary vineyards.

vintner dinner menus

Blanding Residence | 126

California Vegetable Salad with Sauce Ravigote
Monterey Bay Red Abalone with White Summer Corn and Winter Black Truffle Vinaigrette
Parsley Root Agnolotti with Herb Roasted Mushrooms and Bacon Shallot Beurre Rouge
Alder Smoked Sonoma Duck with Almond Risotto
Honeysuckle Ice Cream with Roasted Summer Fruits

Booth Residence | 138

Butter Poached Maine Lobster with Smoked Potato Ravioli, Garlic-Infused Spinach and Lobster Nage
Grilled Kobe Tri-tip Trifolata with Shallot Confiture and Sauce Perigourdine
Mushroom Heritage Barley Casserole
Gianduja Chocolate Mousse with Salad of Mixed Berries and Hazelnut Crème Anglaise

Brown Residence | 154

Goat Cheese Blinis with Red Onion Marmalade
Jumbo Lump Crab with Gnocchi, Chanterelle Mushrooms, English Peas and Parmesan Cream
Sautéed Arctic Char with Roasted Fingerling Potatoes, Haricots Verts and Dijon Crème Fraîche
Crème Sophia with Raspberries and Lemon Verbena Sauce

Heinz Residence | 164

Black Cod with Basil and Rose Petal Pesto
Asparagus Folded Lasagna
Granita allo Champagne
Pork Osso Buco with Porchetta Rub
Chocolate Tartufo

Mott Residence | 176

Tuna Tartare with Osetra Caviar, Yuzu Crème Fraîche and Potato Pancakes
Braised Pork Belly and Tempura Crisps with Local Vegetable Salad and Poached Organic Egg
Wild Mushroom Risotto with Aged Reggiano and Black Truffle
American Kobe Beef Filet and Foie Gras with Leek and Goat Cheese Tater Tots
Chilled Passion Fruit Soup with Vanilla Syrup, Pistachio Cookie and Coconut Gelato

Nelson Residence | 188

Sustainable Bigeye Tuna Foie Gras Tourchon with Sea Salt and Riviera Ligure Olive Oil
Pulled Braised Short Ribs with Toasted Potato Gnocchi, Baby Peas and Wild Mushrooms
Herb and Garlic Crusted Rack of Veal
Poached Texas Peaches with Honey Bavarian Mousse, Sable Breton and White Peach Sorbet

Vogel Residence | 204

Braised Leg of Rabbit with Sausage, Garganelli and Red Wine Marinated Huckleberries
Braised Pork Cheeks and Confit Belly with Cauliflower Purée, Romanesco and Chanterelles
Olive Oil Cake with Red Wine Plums and Pluot Sorbet

Guests enjoyed dinner on the Blandings' outdoor terrace with Bald Mountain as the backdrop. Chef Cal's creations—dishes that glorify food when the flavor is at its peak—paired with the wines of Chappellet Winery and DeLille Cellars, made this meal an epicurean's delight.

a selection of recipes from the

Blanding Residence

Hosted by Robert and Gay-Lynn Blanding
Chappellet Vineyard and DeLille Cellars
Chef Cal Stamenov and Pastry Chef Ben Spungin
Master Sommeliers Shayn Bjornholm and Chris Blanchard

salad
California Vegetable Salad
with Sauce Ravigote

2007 DeLille Cellars Chaleur Estate Blanc

starter
Monterey Bay Red Abalone with White Summer Corn
and Winter Black Truffle Vinaigrette

2007 Chappellet Napa Valley Chardonnay

side
Parsley Root Agnolotti with Herb Roasted Mushrooms
and Bacon Shallot Beurre Rouge

2005 Chappellet Syrah
2005 DeLille Cellars Doyenne Syrah

main
Alder Smoked Sonoma Duck
with Almond Risotto

2006 Chappellet Merlot
2005 DeLille Cellars Doyenne AIX

dessert
Honeysuckle Ice Cream
with Roasted Summer Fruits

1998 Chappellet Chenin Blanc Liqueroux

California Vegetable Salad

California Vegetable Salad
with Sauce Ravigote
serves 6

½ pound mustard or arugula leaves, washed and dried

3 to 4 small heirloom tomatoes, quartered

1 watermelon radish, shaved

1 Japanese cucumber, shaved

1 asparagus stalk, shaved

6 baby carrots, peeled

18 yellow French beans

24 Kalamata olives, pitted

2 ounces feta cheese, crumbled

extra virgin olive oil

Sauce Ravigote

2 tablespoons shallots, chopped

2 tablespoons white vinegar

2 tablespoons tarragon vinegar

1 egg yolk

1 teaspoon mustard

½ bunch fresh tarragon leaves, chopped

½ cup olive oil

salt and pepper to taste

preparation. Wash and dry the mustard or arugula leaves and set aside. Quarter the tomatoes. Peel the carrots and set aside. Use a mandoline to shave the radish, cucumber, asparagus, beans and olives. Set aside on a cutting board. If you don't own a mandoline, julienne the vegetables and set aside.

sauce ravigote. Mix vinegars and shallots in a small saucepan over medium heat and reduce until liquid evaporates. Allow to cool, then transfer to an electric mixer. Add egg yolk, mustard and tarragon leaves, then mix for 30 seconds. Slowly add the olive oil to emulsify. Add salt and pepper to taste.

final assembly and plating. Set out six plates for salad. Dividing the sauce ravigote into six servings, use the back of a spoon to create a small circle of sauce in the middle of each plate. Layer and arrange the mustard or arugula leaves, then the vegetables and feta cheese on top of the circle of sauce. Drizzle with olive oil. Serve.

2007 DeLille Cellars Chaleur Estate Blanc: This wine's creamy nose of grapefruit, pineapple and strawberry also has notes of toasted almond and pear.

Monterey Bay Red Abalone

Monterey Bay Red Abalone
with White Summer Corn and Winter Black Truffle Vinaigrette
serves 4

16 abalone, 3 to 3½ inches each (4 per serving)

olive oil

pinch of flour

¼ bunch cilantro leaves

Black Truffle Vinaigrette

1 ounce winter black truffle, thinly sliced

¼ cup button (brown or white) mushrooms, thinly sliced

¼ cup sherry vinegar

5 tablespoons extra virgin olive oil

1 tablespoon hot water, if needed

salt and pepper to taste

Corn Purée

5 ears fresh white corn (or yellow)

1 tablespoon butter

2 tablespoons parmesan cheese, grated (optional)

salt and pepper to taste

preparation. Remove shell, beak, black ink and lips from abalone meat. Place meat between 2 pieces of plastic wrap and pound to tenderize. Coat with olive oil and cilantro, then seal into vacuum bags. Poach at 175°F for 2 hours 30 minutes. While the abalone is poaching, prepare the black truffle vinaigrette and corn purée. After poaching, remove abalone from vacuum bag. Season with salt and pepper and sprinkle with flour. Sear in olive oil over medium heat until golden in color.

black truffle vinaigrette. Combine the sliced truffles (Tuber melansporum), mushrooms, vinegar, salt and pepper in a small saucepan and cook over medium heat until the sherry just comes to a boil. Transfer to a blender or mini food processor and purée until very smooth. If using a blender, add the oil in a slow, steady stream on the lowest speed. If using a mini food processor, add oil slowly through the feed tube. If the purée is too thick, add a tablespoon of hot water. Taste and adjust seasoning.
Transfer the vinaigrette to a plastic squeeze bottle. The vinaigrette will keep, refrigerated, for three months. Yields ½ cup.

corn purée. Clean corn. Using a sharp knife, run the blade down the center of each kernel, cutting each kernel in half. Holding the cob in one hand and using the back of the knife (30° angle), scrape the juice and germ into a large flat pan (can be messy) until all that is remaining is the skin of each kernel. (Save kernels from one ear of corn and to mix with the purée for texture.)
Heat mixture in a small saucepan. Add 1 tablespoon butter, salt and pepper to taste. Add parmesan cheese, if desired. Cook to a thick consistency, approximately 5 minutes. Add reserved kernels.

final assembly and plating. Spoon corn onto plates. Place red abalone on top. Drizzle with black truffle vinaigrette. If desired, garnish with cilantro.

2007 Chappellet Napa Valley Chardonnay: This enticing Chardonnay begins with tropical fruit aromatics alongside fragrant floral notes and hints of toast and yeast.

Parsley Root Agnolotti

Parsley Root Agnolotti
with Herb Roasted Mushrooms and Bacon Shallot Beurre Rouge
serves 4 to 6

1 cup trumpet or porcini mushrooms

1 cup chanterelle or hedgehog mushrooms

3 tablespoons olive oil, divided

2 tablespoons shallots, minced

1 clove garlic, minced

2 teaspoons fresh Italian parsley, minced

2 teaspoons fresh tarragon, minced

2 teaspoons fresh thyme, minced

salt and pepper to taste

Bacon Shallot Beurre Rouge

3 pieces applewood smoked bacon, chopped

1 cup dry red wine

½ cup red wine vinegar

½ cup shallots, minced

3 fresh tarragon sprigs

½ teaspoon whole black peppercorns

12 tablespoons unsalted butter, cold

salt and pepper to taste

Parsley Root Agnolotti

1 cup cream

2 cups parsley root, roughly chopped

1 teaspoon salt

½ teaspoon pepper

6-8 sheets flat pasta dough (homemade or store-bought)

1 egg

herb roasted mushrooms. Clean the mushrooms with damp paper towels, or use a paring knife to lightly scrape off any loose dirt. If you must wash them, let the mushrooms dry on paper towels or a wire rack for 2 hours in a warm place before proceeding. Trim mushrooms then slice ¼-inch thick.

You can cook the mushrooms up to 2 hours in advance. Place a sauté pan on high heat. When hot, add 1 tablespoon olive oil. Add one variety of mushroom, sprinkling with salt to help them melt and soften. Sauté the mushrooms, without stirring, over high heat until one side begins to color and becomes slightly crusty. Reduce the heat to medium high, and flip the mushrooms to their uncooked side to finish cooking. The length of cooking time will depend on the variety of mushrooms you choose. Remove the cooked mushrooms. Add 1 tablespoon olive oil to pan again and repeat process with the remaining uncooked mushrooms, one variety at a time to preserve distinct flavor and texture. Loosely cover with aluminum foil and set aside at room temperature until ready to use.

bacon shallot beurre rouge. In a small heavy saucepan, lightly brown the bacon. Add the red wine, vinegar, shallots, tarragon and peppercorns. Bring to a boil and cook until reduced to ¼ cup, about 15 minutes. Strain through a fine sieve into another saucepan.

Whisk in the butter, 1 tablespoon at a time, adding each piece just before the previous one has been completely incorporated. Continue until all the butter is incorporated and the sauce coats the back of a spoon. Season to taste with salt and pepper. Set aside until ready to use.

parsley root agnolotti. Combine cream, parsley root, pepper and salt in a small pot. Bring to a simmer for 20 minutes or until parsley root is fork tender. Remove from heat and purée in blender. Adjust seasoning as needed.

Crack egg into small bowl and whisk gently with a fork to combine.

Cut pasta sheets into 4-inch squares. Scoop 1 tablespoon of parsley root purée onto each square. Using a pastry brush, place a thin layer of egg wash on one side of the pasta. Fold the pasta over the dough to seal the agnolotti and press out any air pockets. Use a pastry wheel or cutter to make a clean or crimped edge. The final shape can be square, crescent or round.

Bring a pot of salted water to a boil. Gently add agnolotti and cook for 1 to 2 minutes, or until floating.

Place a large skillet over high heat. When hot, add the remaining tablespoon of olive oil. Combine all of the cooked mushrooms and sauté, stirring frequently, to reheat and crisp the mushrooms, about 2 minutes. Reduce the heat to medium. Add the shallots, garlic, pepper, parsley, tarragon and thyme and stir to combine.

final assembly and plating. Divide agnolotti between 4 to 6 plates. Top with herb roasted mushrooms and drizzle generously with bacon shallot beurre rouge. Serve immediately.

2005 DeLille Cellars Doyenne Syrah: Aromas of white pepper, wild flowers, red apricots and citrus peel are complemented by dense berries and olives in this age-worthy Syrah.

2005 Chappellet Syrah: Exotic pomegranate, grenadine and white pepper create an intriguing invitation. Ripe flavors of fig, plum and dried cherry, with spicy herbal notes that linger.

Alder Smoked Sonoma Duck

Alder Smoked Sonoma Duck
with Almond Risotto
serves 4 to 6

2 to 3 pounds fresh Muscovy ducks, quartered

mesquite or hickory charcoal or wood chips (or 6 rosemary branches), soaked

fresh rosemary sprigs

Almond Risotto

2 tablespoons olive oil

½ medium onion, diced

1 cup carnaroli (or arborio) rice

2 tablespoons toasted almonds, grated on microplane

1 cup white wine

4 cups chicken (or vegetable) stock, heated

8 tablespoons unsalted butter, softened

¼ cup parmesan cheese

advance preparation. Cut the ducks into 4 pieces each (2 legs and 2 breasts). The breasts can be either left on the bone or taken off, skin on. If ordering a duck through your butcher, ask him or her to do this for you. Reserve the carcasses, necks and giblets, if any, for making stock. Season both sides of the duck with salt and pepper.

Prepare a mesquite or hickory charcoal BBQ grill over low heat. If using a gas grill, soak a handful of wood chips for at least 30 minutes, then drain. Poke holes in a small, disposable aluminum foil pan and add the wood chips. Heat the grill on its lowest setting, placing wood chips in the middle of the grill. Alternatively, use 6 wet rosemary branches. These will smoke and eventually burn, imparting a wonderful aroma to the duck.

Place the breasts and legs, skin side down, on the coolest spot of the grill. Cover the grill and slowly smoke the duck for 16 to 20 minutes or less. This will render the fat from the skin, while turning it a beautiful golden brown. Check on the duck once or twice to ensure it is not cooking too quickly. The duck breasts should be undercooked; they will finish cooking at a later stage. Remove breasts from grill. If breasts are on the bone, de-bone them. Cover the duck with aluminum foil and set aside at room temperature for 2 hours.

almond risotto. Heat oil in thick-bottomed saucepan over medium heat. Add onions and cook until translucent. Add rice and almonds and stir slowly. Add wine. Increase heat and bring to a rapid simmer. Stir over rapid simmer for 2 minutes. Stir constantly to ensure even cooking of rice.

Add stock, a little at a time (about ½ cup), keeping a soupy consistency. The whole process should take about 15 to 18 minutes for carnaroli rice (an additional 5 to 10 minutes if cooking at altitude and about 3 to 4 minutes less for arborio). Cook al dente. Add butter and parmesan cheese, stir until melted. Time this to coincide with slicing of the duck.

preparation. Broil the duck in the oven, fat side up, until cooked to desired doneness (5 to 8 minutes for medium-rare). Transfer the duck to a cutting board, and with a sharp knife, slice each breast on a slight diagonal into 4 or 5 pieces.

final assembly and plating. Divide the risotto onto plates and add equal portions of duck on top. Serve. This dish was served at the original vintner dinner with roasted fig.

2005 DeLille Cellars Doyenne AIX: Exhibiting a spicy and floral nose with flavors of black raspberries, blueberries, cherries and black olives, this is a generous and seductive wine.

2006 Chappellet Merlot: A rich, silky and hedonistic Merlot, this wine begins with vibrant aromatics of raspberry and red and black cherry, accented by clove, anise and a hint of pepper.

Honeysuckle Ice Cream

Honeysuckle Ice Cream
with Roasted Summer Fruits
serves 8

6 cups honeysuckle flowers*
(reserve a few for garnish)

2 cups cream

2 cups milk

¾ cup sugar

12 yolks, whisked

assorted seasonal summer berries and stonefruit (peaches, plums, apricots, nectarines, figs)

advance preparation. Combine cream, milk and sugar in a large sauce pot and bring to a boil, stirring frequently. Once boiling, add flowers and whisk for 10 seconds.

Temper the warm cream/milk mixture into the egg yolks (slowly pour into a bowl with the egg yolks while whisking constantly). Strain the mixture through a fine sieve back into the warm sauce pot. Whisk mixture over low heat until it is thick enough to coat the back of a spoon. Strain again and chill in an ice bath. Process in an ice cream maker according to manufacturer's instructions.

preparation. When ice cream is done, prepare roasted berries and summer stonefruit. Cut desired stonefruit in half and remove pits. Spread fruit on baking sheet and sprinkle with granulated sugar. Place fruit under broiler for a few minutes while the sugar caramelizes and the fruit gently cooks.

final assembly and plating. Serve a scoop or two of honeysuckle ice cream topped with warm fruit.

NOTE: This recipe requires an ice cream maker.

*To purchase honeysuckle flowers, see sources on page 234.

 1998 Chappellet Chenin Blanc Liqueroux: Enticing scents of fig, honey and tropical fruits are balanced with great acidity and a lingering flavor of apricot, peach, mango and lemons.

At the Booths' home on the banks of the Big Wood River, guests enjoyed an unforgettable evening beneath the stars. The night attained perfection with a mixture of Cardinale's fine wines, Chef Taki's delectable foods and a warm and welcoming home filled with friends and a visit from a neighborhood moose.

a selection of recipes from the

Booth Residence

Hosted by Debbe and Spike Booth
Cardinale, Hartford Family Winery, La Jota Vineyard Co.
Chef Constantinos "Taki" Laliotitis

starter
Butter Poached Maine Lobster
with Smoked Potato Ravioli, Garlic-Infused Spinach
and Lobster Nage

2008 Hartford Court Stone Côte Chardonnay

main
Grilled Kobe Tri-tip Trifolata
with Shallot Confiture and Sauce Perigourdine

2006 Cardinale

side
Mushroom Heritage Barley Casserole

dessert
Gianduja Chocolate Mousse
with Salad of Mixed Berries and Hazelnut Crème Anglaise

2006 Hartford Court Late Harvest Zinfandel

Butter Poached Maine Lobster

Butter Poached Maine Lobster
with Smoked Potato Ravioli, Garlic-Infused Spinach and Lobster Nage
serves 6

3 whole Maine lobsters

1 cup white wine vinegar

1 cup kosher salt

4 vine ripe tomatoes, quartered

1 onion, quartered

3 carrots, halved lengthwise
and sliced ½-inch thick

1 bunch tarragon

1 cup heavy cream

micro herbs
(chervil or fennel fronds)

Smoked Potato Ravioli

(recipe and ingredients
on next page)

Garlic-Infused Spinach

(recipe and ingredients
on next page)

Butter Poaching Sauce

(recipe and ingredients
on next page)

advance preparation. Fill a 3-gallon pot with water and bring to a boil. Euthanize the lobster by placing the tip of a chef's knife into the head of the lobster. Immediately place lobsters into another large pot with room to cover them with the boiling water. Pour the vinegar and salt into the boiling water and then immediately pour the water over the lobsters. Allow the lobster to par-cook for approximately 2 minutes. Separate the claws, knuckles and tail from each lobster, remove the tail meat and rinse and refrigerate. Remove claws and knuckles also. Separate claws from the knuckles. Place the claws back in the water for 30 seconds, one at a time. After the claw has been warmed up, firmly grab the pincer portion of the claw and pull it out. Using a chef's knife, carefully crack the back end of the claw off. The claw should come right out when shaken. Repeat process with other claws and refrigerate. Using kitchen shears, cut the knuckles out and refrigerate. Trim the feather-like gills along the side of the lobster and cut away any of the interior so that all that is left are the legs of the lobster. Be careful not to trim too much, as this is where all the flavor of the lobster is. Cut the lobster down the center. Place it in a bowl and rinse until the water runs clear.

lobster nage. Best if made a day in advance. Place the lobster bodies, tomatoes, onions, carrots and tarragon in a pot. Cover with water and bring to a simmer. Cook at a gentle simmer for 1 hour and 20 minutes. Pour the stock through a colander placed in a large bowl. Using a wooden kitchen spoon, vigorously crush the lobster bodies and tomatoes against the side of the colander to extract all liquid. It is very important to crush the lobsters into very small, fine pieces. Once the lobsters are dry, they can be discarded. Pour lobster stock through a fine sieve back into the pot. Reduce until you have approximately ⅓ cup of liquid (anywhere from 1 to 1½ hours). This liquid is called glace and is a very concentrated lobster essence. Be sure to strain several times throughout the reduction process. Pour through the fine sieve again, gently tapping the side of the sieve to pass the glace. Place the glace in a small pot and add the cream. Bring to a simmer and cook for 4 minutes. The final yield should be 1¼ cups. Season with salt and refrigerate.

preparation. Prepare the smoked potato ravioli (recipe on next page). While the ravioli are in the refrigerator, prepare the garlic-infused spinach (recipe on next page) and the butter poaching sauce (recipe on next page).

final assembly and plating. Poach the lobster in the butter poaching sauce according to recipe on the next page. While the lobster is poaching, boil ravioli until done, about 2 minutes (they will rise to the top). Place ravioli in a bowl and toss with a little bit of the butter sauce to keep them from sticking. Cover and set aside. Place spinach in the microwave and heat for 1 minute. Bring lobster reduction to a quick simmer and process it with a hand blender.
Once all the ingredients are ready, plate a small pile of spinach. Place the ravioli on top of the spinach, followed by a little more spinach, then the lobster tail and claw. Spoon the lobster sauce around the ravioli, garnish with micro herbs. Serve.

2008 Hartford Court Stone Côte
Chardonnay: Floral and white
peach aromas with notes of
crystallized ginger.

Garlic-Infused Spinach

Butter Poached Maine Lobster
with Smoked Potato Ravioli, Garlic-Infused Spinach and Lobster Nage
(continued from page 141)

Smoked Potato Ravioli

2 russet potatoes, peeled and cut into eighths

3 tablespoons butter

½ cup cream

1 teaspoon liquid smoke (as needed)

6 to 8 sheets of flat pasta

1 egg

salt and pepper to taste

Garlic-Infused Spinach

10 garlic cloves, halved

½ cup vegetable oil

1 tablespoon butter

8 ounces spinach, washed

1 lemon, zested and juiced

salt to taste

Butter Poaching Sauce

1 pound butter, cubed

3 tablespoons water

smoked potato ravioli. Place potatoes in a large pot and cover with water. Add a pinch of salt and bring to a simmer. Cook potatoes until a small knife inserted into them can be easily removed. Drain then mash the potatoes, yielding about 2½ cups potato purée. Place butter and cream into small sauce pot and bring to a boil. Place mashed potatoes back into pot and whisk in cream and butter mixture. Season with salt and pepper. Add as much liquid smoke as necessary until a mild smoky flavor is reached (approximately 1 teaspoon). Spread the potatoes out onto a platter and chill. To assemble the pasta, use a large (2- to 3-ounce) ice cream scoop to scoop the potato purée directly onto each sheet of pasta, making sure to leave a 1½-inch perimeter around the potatoes. Whisk egg in a bowl and brush pasta with a light layer of egg wash. Take another sheet of pasta, and starting at the left, gently lay the sheet on top of the egg-washed sheet and over the domes of potato. Press down from top to bottom to eliminate air bubbles in the ravioli. With the tips of your fingers, press down on the pasta to ensure a good seal. Using a ring-shaped cutter (or a kitchen knife), cut the ravioli out of the sheet. Refrigerate.

garlic-infused spinach. Preheat oven to 300°F. Place garlic in a small oven-proof saucepan. Add oil and bring to a simmer. Place in oven and allow to cook for about 10 minutes. While garlic oil is in the oven, place a large sauté pan over medium heat and add butter. Once butter is melted, add half of the garlic cloves and 1 teaspoon of the garlic oil from the oven. When the butter starts to sizzle and foam, add spinach. Stir continuously. Season with a pinch of salt, half of the lemon zest and a dash of lemon juice. Continue stirring until the spinach has wilted completely. Pour out onto a platter and refrigerate.

butter poaching sauce. Pour 3 tablespoons of water into a 3- or 4-quart saucepan. Bring to a boil and put pan off to the side. After 1 minute, add 3 to 4 cubes of butter into pan with the water and begin to whisk. Once the butter starts to melt, place pan back over the burner on low. Continue adding the butter and whisking it in until you have used all the butter. Keep the butter sauce over low heat at a temperature of 140°F. Season the lobster tails with salt and drop into the butter. Make sure to keep the temperature at 140°F. Cook for approximately 10 minutes or just until the lobster is firm to the touch and begins to curl.

Grilled Kobe Tri-Tip Trifolata

Grilled Kobe Tri-Tip Trifolata
with Shallot Confiture and Sauce Perigourdine
serves 6

2½ pounds Kobe tri-tip

3 garlic cloves, crushed and chopped into a paste

2 tablespoons fresh thyme, chopped

2 tablespoons fresh parsley, chopped

¼ cup vegetable oil

salt and pepper to taste

Shallot Confiture

4 tablespoons butter

2 cups shallots, minced

2 tablespoons fresh thyme, minced

salt and pepper to taste

Sauce Perigourdine

1 tablespoon butter

1 tablespoon truffle, diced

3 tablespoons Madeira

½ cup veal demi-glace

¼ teaspoon black truffle oil

salt to taste

advance preparation. Place the beef onto a cutting board and cut the loin-like muscle from the triangular piece. These are two different muscles and need to be cooked and cut differently. In a storage container, mix the garlic clove paste, thyme, parsley and vegetable oil, then rub into the beef. Cover. Marinate in refrigerator for 24 hours. (The mushroom heritage barley casserole should also be prepared in advance. See recipe on next page.)

preparation. Allow the tri-tip to sit at room temperature for at least 1 hour. If serving with the mushroom heritage barley casserole (recipe on next page), also allow the barley mixture to sit at room temperature for a minimum of 1 hour. Preheat grill to 350°F.

shallot confiture. In a small pot, melt 4 tablespoons butter over low heat. Once melted, add the shallots and thyme. Cover and cook on low for 30 minutes, stirring constantly. Shallots should be translucent and very soft. Salt and pepper to taste. Cover and refrigerate until ready to plate. (Use excess in any dish to add a sweet, complex, earthy flavor.)

sauce perigourdine. Melt 1 tablespoon butter in a small sauce pot over medium heat. Sauté the truffle for approximately 1 minute and add half of the Madeira. Reduce the wine to almost dry and add the demi-glace. Bring to a simmer, skimming off any foam that rises to the top. Add the remainder of the Madeira. Season with salt if necessary. Keep warm and set aside. If serving with the mushroom heritage barley casserole, finish the last steps of the barley recipe in the preheated oven as directed (see recipe on next page).

kobe tri-tip. Season the beef with salt and pepper. Grill over medium to high heat. Once the steaks are well-grilled, move to the low- to medium-heated area of the grill and cook steaks to desired temperature. Remove steaks from grill and allow to rest for a minimum of 5 minutes.

final assembly and plating. Heat the shallot confiture in small saucepan and, just before serving, whisk in the truffle oil. Slice the beef into thick medallions (approximately 5 ounces per person). Spoon on the shallot confiture and pour the warm sauce perigourdine around the beef. Serve with the mushroom heritage barley casserole if desired.

 2006 Cardinale: The 2006 harmonizes tones of each vineyard source. Its dark fruit and minerality is enhanced by traces of freshly brewed coffee and cassis.

Mushroom Heritage Barley Casserole

Mushroom Heritage Barley Casserole
serves 6

1 quart button cap mushrooms, washed and sliced

1 sprig fresh thyme

1 tablespoon butter

1 cup freshly shucked corn

1 teaspoon fresh rosemary, chopped

1 cup dried porcini

1 tablespoon vegetable oil

2 shallots, minced

1 cup heritage variety barley (or substitute regular barley)

¼ cup parmesan cheese, finely grated

¼ cup fresh parsley, chopped

1 lemon, juiced

salt and pepper to taste

preparation. Place the button cap mushrooms into a large soup pot and cover with approximately 12 cups water. Add thyme sprig and bring to a simmer. Simmer for 1½ hours, skimming off any foam that rises to the top. Strain through a fine sieve and place back into the pot over high heat. Reduce the mushroom stock to approximately 3½ cups.

While stock is cooking, prepare the corn. Using a sharp knife, run the blade down the edge of the cob, separating the whole kernels from the cob. Place sauté pan over medium-high heat. Melt the butter in the pan and add corn kernels. Season with salt and the rosemary. Cook the corn for approximately 2 minutes then pour onto a plate.

Place the dried porcini mushrooms in a bowl. Pour 2 cups of boiling water over the mushrooms and allow to steep for 30 minutes. Remove mushrooms from water. Strain this water through a fine sieve into the mushroom stock. This will add more mushroom flavor. Coarsely chop the mushrooms and mix with the corn on the plate. Place another soup pot over medium heat. Add vegetable oil and shallots. Cook for about 2 minutes or until slightly translucent. Add barley and continue cooking until slightly toasted. Add 3 cups mushroom stock and bring to a simmer. Cover and reduce heat to low. Cook until tender but with a bit of firmness left in the grain. If it is crunchy or starchy, it is still undercooked. If it is dry but undercooked, add remaining mushroom stock. You should have ½ cup of mushroom stock remaining to make any corrections.

When barley is at the desired doneness, fold in the corn, mushrooms, cheese and parsley. If desired, add more cheese, herbs or butter. Adjust seasoning with lemon juice, salt and pepper.

Portion the barley into 6- to 8-ounce ramekins or one large casserole dish. Sprinkle with a little cheese and reserve at room temperature for 1 hour before using, or in refrigerator if preparing in advance. Remember to remove from the refrigerator at least 1 hour prior to heating (it must be room temperature before putting into the oven).

final assembly and plating. Preheat oven to 350°F. Place ramekins of barley onto a cookie sheet and place into the oven. Cook until the tops of the barley turn golden brown (approximately 20 minutes). This may vary depending on calibration of the oven, altitude and location of the rack. Once golden brown, remove from the oven and allow to cool. Serve with grilled Kobe tri-tip trifolata (recipe from previous page).

Gianduja Chocolate Mousse

Gianduja Chocolate Mousse
with Salad of Mixed Berries and Hazelnut Crème Anglaise
serves 8

12 ounces Gianduja chocolate, (or other quality chocolate) chopped into small pieces

2 egg yolks

2 tablespoons sugar

½ cup heavy cream

1 teaspoon Knorr granulated gelatin, bloomed in cold water and squeezed out

2 cups heavy cream, whipped to soft peaks

Devil's Food Cake

1 cup flour

1 cup sugar

⅓ cup cocoa powder

1 teaspoon baking powder

1 teaspoon kosher salt

1 large egg

½ cup buttermilk

8 tablespoons melted butter

1 teaspoon vanilla extract

½ cup boiling water

Chocolate Tuile

(recipe and ingredients on next page)

Salad of Mixed Berries

(recipe and ingredients on next page)

Hazelnut Crème Anglaise

(recipe and ingredients on next page)

advance preparation. Place the chocolate into a metal bowl and cover with plastic wrap. Make a double boiler by simmering no more than 1 cup of water in a sauce pot and placing the metal bowl with the chocolate over it. This will melt the chocolate slowly.

In another bowl, whisk together the yolks and sugar and set aside. Scald cream in a small sauce pot, and then pour over egg and sugar mixture. Whisk thoroughly. Pour cream, egg and sugar mixture back into the pot and place the pot over medium heat. Stir constantly, until mixture thickens and coats the back of a spoon (or if using a digital thermometer, when at 168°F).

Add bloomed gelatin into hot egg mixture and stir until melted. Quickly pour the hot egg mixture through a fine sieve and right onto the melting chocolate. Stir until mixture is well incorporated and chocolate has melted completely. Remove the bowl of chocolate from over the pot and bring to room temperature.

Once the chocolate has cooled to the touch, add 1 cup of whipped cream into the chocolate mixture and stir well. Then fold the chocolate and cream mixture back into the other cup of cold whipped cream. Transfer to an airtight container and store in the refrigerator until ready to use.

Prepare the chocolate tuile (recipe on next page) and hazelnut crème anglaise (recipe on next page), and set aside until ready to use.

preparation. Preheat the oven to 300°F.

Prepare the berry salad (recipe on next page). While the berry mixture is allowed to macerate, bake the devil's food cake. Grease and lightly flour a 9 x 13-inch baking sheet. In the bowl of an electric mixer fitted with the paddle attachment, sift together flour, sugar, cocoa, baking powder and salt.

In a small bowl, mix together the egg, buttermilk and melted butter. Pour into mixing bowl and mix on slow until well incorporated. Add boiling water and mix on high until batter is smooth.

Pour batter into floured baking sheet and bake for 45 minutes. Cake is done when the tip of a knife or toothpick inserted into center of cake comes out clean. Allow to chill. Once well chilled, remove from pan and cut into circles measuring 2½ inches in diameter (so that it will fit inside the chocolate tuile rings, recipe on next page).

final assembly and plating. Place a piece of devil's food cake onto the center of a plate. Gently place the chocolate tuile ring around the cake. Remove the mousse from the refrigerator and place into a piping bag. (If you do not have a piping bag, use a plastic bag with one corner cut off.) Pipe the chocolate mousse into the ring on top of the cake, but against the sides of the ring so that it will form a well in the center. If done properly, the mousse will trap the sweet berry juices and moisten the cake below, but not allow them to run onto the plate. The mousse should not come over the edge of the toile ring.

Mix the berry salad and place a spoonful of berries into the center of the ring, piled up in a perfect mound. Serve the hazelnut sauce in a saucier or drizzle directly onto the plate. Garnish with tiny mint leaves and serve immediately.

 2006 Hartford Court Late Harvest Zinfandel: With a nose of black fruits interlaced with candied orange zest and anise, this "Port" finishes with the flavor and texture of a chocolate cake.

Salad of Mixed Berries

Gianduja Chocolate Mousse
with Salad of Mixed Berries and Hazelnut Crème Anglaise
(continued from page 149)

Chocolate Tuile

1 tablespoon flour

4 tablespoons cocoa powder

1 cup sugar

2-3 egg whites (⅓ cup)

7 tablespoons butter,
at room temperature

Salad of Mixed Berries

1 pint raspberries

1 pint blackberries, cut in half

½ cup blueberries

1 cup strawberries,
quartered if large

3 tablespoon powdered sugar

2 tablespoon Chambord
or other appropriate liqueur

Hazelnut Crème Anglaise

1 cup whole milk

½ cup heavy cream

½ vanilla bean

1 orange, zested

5 egg yolks

5 tablespoons sugar

6 tablespoons Frangelico
liqueur

chocolate tuile. Preheat oven to 350°F.

In a bowl, mix all dry ingredients together. Add egg whites and mix well, followed by soft butter. Allow to rest for 20 minutes.

On a non-stick silicone baking mat using an offset spatula, spread a thin layer of the mixture over a rectangular cut stencil no thicker than ¹⁄₁₆ inch and measuring 1 inch by 10½ inches. Stencil can be made from silicone baking sheets or large plastic lids from yogurt containers. Repeat this stencil and spreading action several times. The goal is to make long rectangular chocolate strips to later be shaped into rings.

Place silicone mat on top shelf of oven and bake for 6 minutes. Quickly remove from oven and carefully pull the strips off mat. Using a chef's knife, trim edges of tuile to make them straight and clean. Place back on mat and cook for another 3 minutes. Remove from oven, and using a round cutter or mold measuring 2¾ inches in diameter, wrap the tuile around mold and allow to cool. Repeat this process until you have the desired number of servings.

salad of mixed berries. Mix all ingredients into a bowl and refrigerate. Allow to macerate for a minimum of 1 hour.

hazelnut crème anglaise. In a 2-quart sauce pot, combine the milk and cream. Cut the vanilla bean in half lengthwise and scrape out the insides. Put the pulp of the bean along with the bean into the milk and cream mixture with the orange zest. Bring to a simmer over medium heat.

While waiting for milk to simmer, whisk the egg yolks and sugar together. When milk is simmering, slowly pour the milk into the egg and sugar mixture, whisking continuously. Pour the milk and egg mixture back into the pot and add the liqueur. Cook over low to medium heat until mixture thickens and coats the back of a spoon (or if using a digital thermometer, when at 168°F). Pour through a fine sieve and into a metal bowl sitting in an icy bath. Chill promptly and refrigerate.

style tips

Outdoor dining can still be elegant and stylish. Colorful plastic goblets, pitchers and dinnerware add pattern and style. Organically inspired and floral-themed centerpieces and napkin rings help to add elegance to any outdoor setting.

picnic in style

Plastic dinnerware—you've come a long way baby! Outdoor dining by the river or at a picturesque picnic spot doesn't mean you have to sacrifice style. There's a large variety of plastic goblets, pitchers and dinnerware available to dress up your table settings with color and pattern. Don't be afraid to mix and match. *Courtesy Bellissimo.*

summer flowers

Historically considered only as spring bulbs, tulips can now be found year-round. Their vibrant colors and varied shapes make them perfect cut flowers, ideal to add contrast to traditional summer blooms such as pink garden roses, sunflowers, yellow freesia and pink hydrangeas. *Courtesy Taylor'd Events.*

napkins and flowers

Dress up any table setting by adding a sprig of herbs or flowers to your napkins. Rosemary, lavender and Gerbera daisies work well because they can withstand the lack of water and also add a fragrant note to the setting. Cut the entire stem off and set the head in the middle of the folded napkin. *Courtesy Bellissimo.*

The Browns' eclectic house sits near the flowing Big Wood River. Guests dined on the patio surrounded by stunning flower gardens and enjoyed the soothing sounds of the river. Chef Sue Zemanick's distinctive, modern cuisine was accompanied by Domaine Serene's Pinot Noirs, as well as Cabernet Sauvignons, Merlots, and Sangioveses from Leonetti Cellar.

a selection of recipes from the

Brown Residence

Hosted by Rufus and Liz Brown,
Pat Aluisi and Donna Solimene
Domaine Serene and Leonetti Cellar
Chef Sue Zemanick

starter
Goat Cheese Blinis
with Red Onion Marmalade

Domaine Serene "R" Rose

side
Jumbo Lump Crab with Gnocchi, Chanterelle
Mushrooms, English Peas and Parmesan Cream

2007 Domaine Serene Côte Sud Vineyard Chardonnay

main
Sautéed Arctic Char with Roasted Fingerling Potatoes,
Haricots Verts and Dijon Crème Fraîche

2006 Domaine Serene Evenstad Reserve Pinot Noir

dessert
Crème Sophia with Raspberries
and Lemon Verbena Sauce

Goat Cheese Blinis

Goat Cheese Blinis
with Red Onion Marmalade
serves 8 to 10

½ cup goat cheese, soft

1 cup all-purpose flour

½ teaspoon baking powder

1 teaspoon salt

2 eggs, beaten

6 tablespoons milk

3 tablespoons chives, minced

2 tablespoons canola oil

Red Onion Marmalade

2 tablespoons canola oil

2 red onions, minced

1 blood orange, juice and zest

½ cup orange juice

2 tablespoons honey

2 tablespoons rice wine vinegar

1 tablespoon grenadine

2 tablespoons red wine vinegar

2 tablespoons red wine

½ teaspoon kosher salt

¼ teaspoon black pepper

⅛ teaspoon ground coriander

⅛ teaspoon ground fennel

pinch of red pepper flakes

red onion marmalade. In a medium sauce pot heat up to 2 tablespoons of canola oil over medium-high heat. Sauté the onions for 3 minutes or until soft. Add all the other ingredients and cook for 10 to 15 minutes until the liquid is almost completely evaporated. Transfer the marmalade to a baking pan to cool completely.

preparation. Prepare blinis. Sift flour, baking powder and salt together in a small mixing bowl. Gradually stir in eggs and milk, then gently fold in 2 tablespoons chives (reserving the rest for garnish). Heat a medium-sized nonstick sauté pan over low heat. Add canola oil to the pan. Working in batches, spoon a teaspoon of the blini batter into the sauté pan. Heat until bubbles start appearing, about 1 minute. Turn and brown on the other side, cooking for 1 minute longer. Remove from the pan and set aside on a baking sheet.

final assembly and plating. Place blinis on a platter. Gently spoon a small amount of goat cheese onto each blini. Then spoon ¼ teaspoon of red onion marmalade on top of goat cheese. Garnish with chives. Serve immediately.

Domaine Serene "R" Rosé: Flavors of cherries, raspberries and a hint of sage impart a creamy richness, while texture and grip from the soil create a lasting, full-bodied finish.

Jumbo Lump Crab with Gnocchi

Jumbo Lump Crab with Gnocchi,
Chanterelle Mushrooms, English Peas and Parmesan Cream
serves 6

1 pound jumbo lump crab

¼ cup clarified butter or canola oil

1 cup chanterelle mushrooms, quartered

1 tablespoon shallots, minced

1 tablespoon garlic, minced

1 teaspoon fresh thyme, chopped

1 cup heavy cream

⅓ cup parmesan cheese, grated

½ teaspoon kosher salt

¼ teaspoon black pepper

½ cup English peas

Gnocchi

1½ pounds Idaho potatoes

1 cup all-purpose flour

1 egg

1 teaspoon kosher salt

canola oil

gnocchi. Prepare in advance. Preheat oven to 375°F. Bake the potatoes for 1 hour or until tender. In a large pot bring 6 cups of water to a boil. Set up an ice bath with 3 cups of water and 3 cups of ice.

While the potatoes are still warm, peel them and run them through a food mill onto a cutting board dusted with flour. Make a well with the potatoes and sprinkle flour over them. Break the egg into the center of the well, add the salt, and mix with a fork to make a dough. Once the dough is formed, knead for 2 minutes. Divide the dough into 3 balls. Roll each ball into a rope ¾-inch in diameter. Cut the rope into 1-inch pieces. Gently drop the gnocchi into the boiling water and cook for 1 minute or until they rise to the surface. Remove gnocchi with a slotted spoon and transfer to the ice bath until they are cool. Drain and toss to coat with canola oil. Set aside. The gnocchi can be stored covered in the refrigerator for 2 days.

preparation. Heat the clarified butter in a large sauté pan over medium-high heat. Just before it starts smoking, add gnocchi and mushrooms. Sauté until golden brown, about 3 minutes.

Drain excess butter from the pan. Add shallots, garlic and thyme, cook for 30 seconds. Then add the cream, parmesan cheese and salt and pepper. Reduce this mixture for 1 minute or until it thickens. To finish, add the peas and the crab, heat through for 1 minute.

final assembly and plating. Spoon onto plates and serve.

2007 Domaine Serene Côte Sud Vineyard Chardonnay: Aromas of tangerine, jasmine, spearmint, pear, spiced apple and vanilla join a palate of ripe apricot, green apple, kiwi, toast and caramel with well-balanced acidity.

Sautéed Artic Char

Sautéed Arctic Char
with Roasted Fingerling Potatoes, Haricots Verts and Dijon Crème Fraîche
serves 6

6 six-ounce Arctic char filets

1 pound fingerling potatoes

1 pound slender green beans (haricots verts)

2 tablespoons shallots, minced

2 tablespoons garlic, chopped

2 tablespoons thyme, chopped

2 tablespoons extra virgin olive oil

2 tablespoons unsalted butter

¼ cup canola oil

salt and pepper to taste

Dijon Crème Fraîche

½ cup crème fraîche

¼ cup Dijon mustard

salt and pepper to taste

dijon crème fraîche. In a small mixing bowl, combine the crème fraîche and Dijon mustard. Season with a pinch of salt and pepper. Prepare in advance and set aside.

preparation. Preheat oven to 375°F. Wash the fingerling potatoes and cut in half lengthwise. In a bowl, toss the potatoes with the olive oil, 1 teaspoon of kosher salt and ½ teaspoon black pepper. Lay the potatoes flat side down on a baking sheet. Place in oven for 10 minutes. Set aside.

In a large soup pot, bring 6 cups of water and 2 tablespoons of salt to a rapid boil. Cook the green beans for 1½ minutes in the boiling water. Remove with a slotted spoon and set aside.

Season the fish filets with 1 teaspoon salt and ½ teaspoon pepper. In a large sauté pan over a high flame, heat canola oil. Gently place each piece of fish in the pan. Cook over high heat for 2 minutes. Flip fish over and turn off the heat.

In a large sauté pan over medium heat, melt 2 tablespoons of butter. Add the shallots, garlic and thyme, cook for 30 seconds, then add the potatoes and green beans. Sauté for 2 minutes.

final assembly and plating. Place the roasted fingerling potatoes and green beans on a plate. Spoon the Dijon crème fraîche around the vegetables and place the fish on top and drizzle with a bit more Dijon crème frâiche. Serve.

2006 Domaine Serene Evenstad Reserve Pinot Noir: A violet and lavender perfume is balanced by summer berries. The palate journeys from luscious fruit to vanilla cola, with hints of dark chocolate and tar.

Creme Sophia

Crème Sophia
with Raspberries and Lemon Verbena Sauce
serves 10

1 vanilla bean

1¾ cup heavy cream

¾ cup milk

6 eggs

6 egg yolks

1 cup sugar, divided

4 lemons

2 tablespoons unsalted butter

2 pints raspberries for garnish

Lemon Verbena Sauce

1 cup sugar

1 cup water

1 cup lemon verbena leaves*

1 vanilla bean, seeds scraped

lemon verbena sauce. In a small sauce pot over low heat, combine the sugar, water, lemon verbena leaves and vanilla bean and simmer until it reaches a syrupy consistency, about 15 minutes. Strain through a fine mesh sieve. Prepare in advance and set aside. You can keep this sauce refrigerated for up to one month.

preparation. Preheat the oven to 300°F. Butter and sugar the ramekins, using 2 tablespoons of sugar. Set them into a shallow baking dish.
Zest all 4 lemons and squeeze juice from 3 lemons. Set aside.
In a medium-sized saucepan, scald the milk, cream and vanilla bean. Turn off the heat and infuse for 5 minutes. In a medium-sized mixing bowl, whisk together the whole eggs, yolks and sugar (1 cup minus 2 tablespoons). Whisk milk and cream mixture into the eggs then add the lemon juice and zest. Pass this mixture through a fine mesh sieve.
Pour this into the ramekins, bake in pan with water bath for 30 to 40 minutes or until set. The water bath should come halfway up the ramekins. Cool overnight before serving.

final assembly and plating. Invert the ramekin into your hand. Give it a good shake to loosen the custard from the sides. Place inverted onto a plate. Garnish with raspberries and drizzle with 1½ tablespoons of lemon verbena sauce.

NOTE: You will need 10 4-ounce ramekins to prepare this dessert.

*Lemon verbena leaves (a type of mint) are available at specialty stores and many farmers markets; see sources on page 234.

At Teresa Heinz and Senator John Kerry's home in Adams Gulch, Allen Shoup of Long Shadows Vintners shared his collection of distinctive wines from Washington state's Columbia Valley. Dawnine and Bill Dyer brought out Meteor Vineyard's vibrant Cabernet Sauvignons and guests were spoiled by the creative cuisine of local favorite Cristina Ceccatelli Cook.

a selection of recipes from the

Heinz Residence

Hosted by Teresa Heinz and Senator John Kerry
Long Shadows Vintners and Meteor Vineyard
Cristina Ceccatelli Cook

starter
Black Cod with Basil and Rose Petal Pesto
(Merluzzo con Pesto di Basilico e Petali di Rose)

2009 Poet's Leap Riesling

side
Asparagus Folded Lasagna
(Lasagna di Asparagi)

2007 *Folonari Saggi*

cleanser
Granita allo Champagne

main
Pork Osso Buco with Porchetta Rub
(Osso Buco di Maiale con Spezie alla Porchetta)

2007 Meteor Cabernet
2005 Meteor Special Family Reserve

dessert
Chocolate Tartufo
(Tartufo al Cioccolato)

2006 Sequel Syrah

Black Cod with Basil and Rose Petal Pesto

Black Cod with Basil and Rose Petal Pesto
(Merluzzo con Pesto di Basilico e Petali di Rose)
serves 6

2 pounds fresh black cod, deboned and cut into 6 pieces, skin on

1 lemon, zested

2 tablespoons lemon juice

5 tablespoons Basil and Rose Petal Pesto (recipe below)

2 tablespoons extra virgin olive oil

salt and pepper to taste

Basil and Rose Petal Pesto

1 cup fresh basil leaves

1 tablespoon pine nuts

6 tablespoons extra virgin olive oil

½ lemon, juiced

petals of 2 yellow and 2 pink roses, about 25 total (reserve a few petals for garnish)

salt and pepper to taste

basil and rose petal pesto. In a food processor, pulse together the basil leaves, pine nuts, 6 tablespoons olive oil and lemon juice until well blended. Add petals and pulse until just blended. Transfer to a bowl and cover until ready to use. In a large baking dish, toss the cod with the lemon juice, zest and 2 tablespoons of pesto. Season with salt and pepper. Cover with plastic wrap and marinate in a cool place for 30 minutes.

preparation. Preheat oven to 500°F. Heat olive oil on medium heat in a large oven-proof sauté pan. Add cod to pan, skin side up, reserving the marinade, and sear for 2 minutes. Turn the fish and sear the other side just enough to give it color, about 2 minutes. Pour the reserved marinade into the pan. Place the pan in the oven on a low rack and bake until flaky, about 4 minutes.

final assembly and plating. Transfer cod to a warm serving platter. Drizzle with remaining basil and rose petal pesto. Garnish with a few rose petals. Serve.

2009 Poet's Leap Riesling: Offers citrus aromas with flavors of ripe melon and peach. A slight sweetness is balanced by its natural acidity and a clean finish.

Asparagus Folded Lasagna

Asparagus Folded Lasagna
(Lasagna di Asparagi)
serves 6

6 quarts water

2 tablespoons salt

1½ pounds small asparagus spears, ends removed

6 thin fresh pasta sheets (10 x 5 inches each)

3 cups béchamel sauce (recipe below)

½ cup Italian parsley, minced

1 cup parmigiano or pecorino sardo maturo, grated

extra virgin olive oil

Béchamel Sauce

8 tablespoons unsalted butter

¼ cup all-purpose flour

3 cups whole milk, warmed

¼ teaspoon salt

pinch of nutmeg

preparation. Preheat oven to 475°F. Bring water to a boil with salt. Prepare a large bowl of ice water.
Blanch asparagus in boiling water for 1 minute. Using tongs, remove asparagus from cooking water, dip into ice water, and set aside to drain.
Cook pasta in asparagus water for 2 minutes. Drain pasta, reserving asparagus/pasta water.

béchamel sauce. Melt butter over low heat in a medium saucepan. Whisk in flour and blend until smooth, about 3 to 4 minutes. Add the warm milk, whisking continuously, until mixture is very smooth. Bring to a simmer, then remove from heat and season with salt and nutmeg.
In a large mixing bowl, combine béchamel sauce with 1 cup asparagus/pasta water and parsley. Set aside.

lasagna. Lightly coat cookie sheet or baking pan with ½ teaspoon olive oil. Spread 1½ cups béchamel sauce evenly on bottom.
Place pasta sheets on a flat surface. Arrange 4 to 5 asparagus spears on ⅓ of each sheet, then drizzle with béchamel sauce and sprinkle with parmigiano. Fold the empty part of pasta sheet over the asparagus, leaving the tips of the asparagus showing. Fold pasta back and forth, draping it like a ruffle. Repeat with remaining sheets. (See photo.)
With a spatula, carefully transfer folded lasagnas onto cookie sheet or baking pan. Drizzle with béchamel and sprinkle with parmigiano. Bake until top bubbles and turns golden, about 7 to 8 minutes.

final assembly and plating. Serve with a little béchamel (about 2 tablespoons) on the bottom of each bowl, add folded lasagna, then drizzle additional béchamel on top.

2007 Folonari Saggi: The 2007 features delicate notes of wild strawberry and wood spice. It is silky in texture with a lengthy finish and a slight earthiness.

Pork Osso Buco with Porchetta Rub

Pork Osso Buco with Porchetta Rub
(Osso Buco di Maiale con Spezie alla Porchetta)
serves 6

6 center-cut pork hindshanks osso buco, 2 inches thick (approximately ¾ pound each)

kitchen twine for tying shanks

2 tablespoons porchetta rub (recipe below)

½ cup extra virgin olive oil

2 white onions, cut in ¼-inch thick slices

2 cups white wine

3 large whole cloves garlic

4 bay leaves

6 cups chicken stock

4 to 5 cups water (to cover)

salt and pepper to taste

Porchetta Rub

1 tablespoon fennel seeds

1 tablespoon black peppercorns

1 tablespoon red pepper flakes

1 tablespoon salt

4 cloves garlic, minced (optional)

porchetta rub. Prepare in advance. In a sauté pan, toast fennel seeds over medium heat until slightly darkened and fragrant. Transfer to a food mill and let cool. Add peppercorns, red pepper flakes and salt and grind to a medium consistency. If you are using garlic, add only to the amount you will use immediately.
Store remaining rub in a jar to be used later on chicken, fish or any meat you wish.

advance preparation. Tie each shank with kitchen twine to secure meat to the bone. Rub on all sides with 1½ tablespoons porchetta rub. Refrigerate at least 2 hours or overnight.

preparation. Preheat oven to 350°F. Heat 2 tablespoons olive oil over medium-high heat in a wide sauté pan. Add shanks and brown on all sides, about 10 minutes. Remove shanks and reserve. Add wine to meat juices and reduce on high heat for 1 minute to deglaze the pan. Remove from heat and set aside.
In a separate sauté pan, heat remaining olive oil. Add onions, salt and pepper, and cook on medium heat, stirring occasionally, until golden and translucent, about 15 minutes.
Arrange onions in a single layer in a 9 x 12 x 3½-inch baking dish. Add pork shanks, along with deglazed wine and cooking juices. Add garlic, bay leaves, chicken stock and enough water to cover the meat.
Cover the baking dish securely with aluminum foil and bake on lower rack for 5 to 5½ hours or until meat is falling off the bone. (Check after 3½ hours.) Add hot water or hot chicken stock if necessary, so liquid still covers the meat.

final assembly and plating. Transfer the cooked meat with a little juice and some onions to a serving platter. Carefully cut off the kitchen twine and discard. Keep the meat warm while you heat the remaining juices on high heat until reduced by half. Pour juices over the meat, sprinkle with remaining ½ tablespoon of porchetta rub, and serve.

2007 Meteor Cabernet and 2005 Meteor Special Family Reserve: Aromas of black raspberry with hints of chocolate and espresso highlight the ripe berry fruit and classic styling of these two wines.

Granita allo Champagne

Chocolate Tartufo

Granita allo Champagne
serves 8

1 cup sugar

1 cup water

1 lemon (plus extras for plating)

2 limes

1 bottle Champagne, chilled

preparation. Combine sugar and water in a saucepan. Bring to boil, stirring, until sugar is dissolved. Remove simple syrup from heat and refrigerate 1 hour. With a fine grater, zest skin off lemon and limes, removing only the surface layer. Squeeze juice from both fruits, removing seeds.
Pour Champagne into a 9 x 11 x 2-inch pan. Stir in simple syrup, fruit juices and zest. Place mixture in freezer. Check after 30 minutes. Using a wooden spoon, scrape any ice formed on the sides into the rest of the mixture. Repeat this procedure every hour for 3 to 4 hours, scraping until all liquid is frozen.

final assembly and plating. Before serving, fluff the granita with a wooden spoon, scoop into a juiced lemon and plate. Serve.

NOTE: Serve as a palate cleanser in between courses.

Chocolate Tartufo
(Tartufo al Cioccolato)
serves 6

2 tablespoons water, at room temperature

¼ cup granulated sugar

2 egg yolks

1 tablespoon cocoa powder, sifted (reserve extra for dusting)

½ cup dark chocolate (70% or higher cocoa)

½ teaspoon saba wine syrup*

⅔ cup heavy cream

chocolate sauce (for garnish)

preparation. In a heavy saucepan, dissolve sugar in water over medium-low heat until temperature reaches 108°F.
In the bowl of a stand-up mixer, whip yolks with the sugar/water mixture. Add in cocoa powder.
In a double boiler, melt chocolate with saba wine syrup and set aside.
Fold egg and sugar mixture into melted chocolate.
Whisk cream to soft peaks and fold into chocolate mixture. Refrigerate in bowl overnight or until set, 1 to 2 hours. When ready to serve, line a cookie sheet with parchment paper. Place 6 scoops of chocolate mixture onto the parchment paper and dust with cocoa powder.

final assembly and plating. Transfer scoops onto chilled dessert plates, surround with a drizzle of hot chocolate sauce, and serve.

*For information on where to purchase saba wine syrup, see sources on page 234.

 2006 Sequel Syrah: Complex with a lengthy finish. Almond, dark chocolate and cherry notes mixed with hints of black licorice, blackberry and cocoa powder.

style tip

Embellished napkin rings, decorative plates or textured chargers all add flair and style to table settings. Place cards are another opportunity to get creative and inspire conversation.

stamp cut-outs

Butterfly stamps for a summer luncheon, buckhead stamps for a game dinner—what is your theme? All you need are stamps, inkpads, cardstock and an X-acto (or craft) knife to cut out the stamp shape and create an interesting outline.
Courtesy The Picket Fence.

cork holders

Guest placement is key for great conversation, as well as creating a social and inviting atmosphere. Tie your meal's theme together by using unique place card holders, like wine corks for a wine-focused dinner. Slice one side of the cork so it sits flat, then cut a slit into each cork and insert the place card. *Courtesy The Picket Fence.*

go green

Use fruit to add a simple, yet elegant accent. Green apples or golden pears offer a beautiful shape. Tie each guest's place card around the stem with a colored ribbon or piece of yarn and add an element like a bird's nest placeholder or textured charger to complete the look. *Courtesy The Picket Fence.*

Guests relaxed riverside on the terraces at the Mott residence, where they enjoyed Bordeaux-style wines from Gemstone Vineyards. Ron Lachini of Lachini Vineyards also showcased the winery's small production of Pinot Grigios and dessert wines and Chef Beau MacMillan's food complemented the selections perfectly, with a signature emphasis on innovative, seasonal ingredients.

a selection of recipes from the

Mott Residence

Hosted by Tim Mott and Ann Jones, Tim and Robin Wolff
Gemstone Vineyard and Lachini Vineyards
Chef Beau MacMillan

starter
Tuna Tartare with Osetra Caviar,
Yuzu Crème Fraîche and Potato Pancakes

2008 Lachini Vineyards Family Estate Pinot Noir
2007 Lachini Vineyards Pinot Noir, Cuvée Giselle

salad
Braised Pork Belly and Tempura Crisps
with Local Vegetable Salad and Poached Organic Egg

2006 Lachini Vineyards Library Pinot Noir

side
Wild Mushroom Risotto
with Aged Reggiano and Black Truffle

2007 Facets of Gemstone Estate Red Blend

main
American Kobe Beef Filet and Foie Gras
with Leek and Goat Cheese Tater Tots

2006 Gemstone Estate Cabernet Sauvignon

dessert
Chilled Passion Fruit Soup with Vanilla Syrup,
Pistachio Cookie and Coconut Gelato

2006 Gemstone Estate Cabernet Sauvignon

Tuna Tartare with Osetra Caviar

Tuna Tartare with Osetra Caviar,
Yuzu Crème Fraîche and Potato Pancakes
serves 4

10 ounces sushi-grade ahi tuna, cleaned and diced

4 ounces Osetra caviar

1 bunch green onions, minced

½ cup pine nuts, toasted

4 teaspoons black and white sesame seeds, toasted

1 teaspoon sambal chili paste

1 teaspoon sesame oil

1 teaspoon soy sauce

salt and pepper to taste

1 avocado

4 crispy rice crackers

Yuzu Crème Fraîche

6 tablespoons sour cream

1 tablespoon yuzu juice*

Potato Pancake

10 ounces Idaho baker potatoes, cleaned and peeled

¼ cup flour

1 egg yolk

1 shallot, finely chopped

1 tablespoon vegetable oil

salt and pepper to taste

preparation. Combine diced tuna with green onions, pine nuts, sesame seeds, sambal, sesame oil and soy sauce in a mixing bowl. Season with salt and pepper to taste. Purée avocado in blender or food processor until smooth. Reserve.

yuzu crème fraîche. Combine sour cream and yuzu in a small mixing bowl, and reserve for final plating.

potato pancake. Cube potatoes and place in food processor with shallots. Blend until smooth. Add flour and yolk until mixture is a pancake batter-like consistency. Season with salt and pepper. If the mixture is too loose, add flour; if it is too dense, add another egg yolk.
In a warm non-stick pan, add vegetable oil. Using a tablespoon, spoon batter into pan and cook pancake until crisp on both sides.

final assembly and plating. Press each portion of tuna mixture into a 3-inch ring mold to shape. Spoon a small amount of Osetra caviar on top of tuna. Garnish with a spoonful of yuzu crème fraîche and avocado purée. Place rice cracker in crème fraîche. Serve.

*Yuzu is a Japanese citrus fruit (similar in taste to grapefruit, but with overtones of Mandarin orange), see sources on page 234.

2008 Lachini Vineyards Family Estate Pinot Noir: Dark fruits mingle with floral notes and wild game, all wrapped in vanilla undertones. This full-bodied Chehalem Mountains Pinot Noir has a spicy bouquet and long finish.

2007 Lachini Pinot Noir, Cuvée Giselle: Intense and focused, this wine opens with pungent aromas of forest and clove, tastes of concentrated cranberry and pomegranate fruit and powers through into a full-bodied finish.

Braised Pork Belly and Tempura Crisps

Braised Pork Belly and Tempura Crisps
with Local Vegetable Salad and Poached Organic Egg
serves 4 to 6

1 pound pork belly

1 cup hoisin sauce

8 garlic cloves, chopped

¼ cup salt

⅓ cup ginger, grated

1 cup soy sauce

¾ cup rice wine vinegar

¾ cup sesame oil

4 tablespoons black pepper

2 tablespoons five-spice powder

4 to 6 local organic eggs,
poached (optional)

Local Vegetable Salad

1 bunch kale (or 3 squash
blossoms in season)

1 cup prepared tempura batter

1 pound local mixed lettuce

2 sprigs parsley, picked

2 sprigs cilantro, picked

2 sprigs chives, picked

1 shallot, diced

1 baby carrot, shaved

1 watermelon radish, shaved

1 sheet nori seaweed, julienned

vegetable oil

Soy Sesame Vinaigrette

1 tablespoon vegetable oil

½ tablespoon garlic, minced

½ tablespoon ginger, minced

1 tablespoon green onions,
minced

pinch red chili flakes

½ tablespoon sesame oil

¼ cup rice wine vinegar

¼ cup mirin

¼ cup soy sauce

¼ cup brown sugar

½ teaspoon cornstarch
(dissolved in ¼ cup water)

advance preparation. Preheat oven to 300°F. Combine hoisin sauce, garlic cloves, salt, grated ginger, soy sauce, rice vinegar, sesame oil, black pepper and five-spice powder in a bowl. Mix well, add pork belly and marinate overnight.

preparation. Fill baking dish ⅔ full with chicken stock and bake pork belly with marinade at 300°F for 2 to 3 hours.

soy sesame vinaigrette. Heat vegetable oil in a medium saucepan. Add garlic, ginger, green onion and chili flakes. Sauté until fragrant (about 15 to 20 seconds). Add sesame oil, rice wine vinegar, mirin, soy sauce, brown sugar and cornstarch (dissolved in ¼ cup water). Bring to a boil. Lower heat and simmer until thickened (about 2 to 3 minutes). Strain, cool and set aside.

vegetable salad. While the pork is in the oven, prepare the vegetable salad. Wash and dry lettuce, and set aside. Combine the diced shallot, shaved carrot, radish and seaweed in a small mixing bowl. Add the mixed lettuce, parsley, cilantro and chives and mix. Dress with soy sesame vinaigrette.
Wash the kale. Bring a pot of water to boil and parboil kale briefly until slightly tender (be careful not to overcook or it will become limp). Dry and tear into large pieces, then set aside. Prepare tempura batter according to instructions. Dip kale pieces (or leaves of squash blossom) in tempura batter and deep fry in vegetable oil until golden. Poach the eggs.

final assembly and plating. Arrange vegetable salad in center of each plate. Top with tempura crisps and nori seaweed. Cut the braised pork belly into four portions and sear quickly to add grill marks. Place the pork belly on top of salad and top with the poached egg.

2006 Lachini Vineyards Library Pinot Noir: Dark in color, the nose explodes with an opulent bouquet of wild blackberries, cola, truffle, and toasty oak, accentuated by layers of silky ripe cherries, pomegranate, cassis, crème brûlée and exotic spice notes.

Wild Mushroom Risotto

Wild Mushroom Risotto
with Aged Reggiano and Black Truffle
serves 4 to 6

¾ cup fresh wild mushrooms, chopped (can substitute dried if needed)

2 tablespoons (1 ounce) black truffles, chopped

⅔ cup olive oil

1 parsley bunch, minced

1 medium white onion, chopped

1 pound arborio rice

1 bay leaf

4 cups chicken stock, warmed

2 tablespoons porcini mushroom powder*

½ cup butter

¾ cup parmesan, shredded

2 tablespoons mascarpone

salt and pepper to taste

preparation. In a small saucepan, sauté mushrooms in ⅓ cup olive oil. Add parsley and season with salt and pepper. Set aside.

In a medium heavy-bottomed saucepan, heat the remaining ⅓ cup olive oil over medium-high heat. Add onion and bay leaf and sauté, stirring continuously with a wooden spoon, until just softened, about 3 to 4 minutes. Add rice and continue to stir, using the spoon to coat the rice with oil.

In a separate saucepan, heat the chicken stock until warm. Add chicken stock, one cup at a time, to rice. Continue cooking, stirring often, until liquid is absorbed. Repeat until all stock is used.

Stir in sautéed mushrooms, mushroom powder and chopped truffle. Reduce heat to very low, so that the risotto no longer simmers. Stir in parmesan, mascarpone and butter to offer a creamy finish.

final assembly and plating. Spoon into heated shallow serving bowls. Serve immediately.

NOTE: Dried mushrooms reconstituted in water can replace fresh if wild mushrooms are not available. Reserve mushroom water to add to the stock for a deeper mushroom flavor.

*To purchase porcini mushroom powder, see sources on page 234.

2007 Facets of Gemstone Estate Red Blend: The deep, expressive aromas and flavors are filled with blackberry, fig, sweet cassis, dark cocoa and minerality.

American Kobe Beef Filet and Foie Gras

American Kobe Beef Filet and Foie Gras
with Leek and Goat Cheese Tater Tots
serves 4

4 (6-ounce) Snake River Farms Kobe beef filets

4 applewood-smoked bacon strips

6 ounces foie gras

1 leek, cleaned and chopped (white and light green parts only)

1 pound Idaho baker potatoes

¾ cup milk

4 ounces goat cheese, soft

¾ cup butter

1 tablespoon truffle oil

2 cups panko bread crumbs

3 whole eggs

½ cup petite greens (for final plating)

Merlot Demi-Glace

2 tablespoons vegetable oil

½ pound meat scraps, cut into small pieces

¼ cup shallots

¼ cup garlic

1 bay leaf

1 cup red wine

4 cups chicken stock

salt and pepper to taste

advance preparation. To prepare the leek and goat cheese tater tots, sauté leeks over medium heat until tender.

Clean and peel potatoes, then cut into 1-inch cubes. Place cubes in saucepan with milk. Season with salt and pepper and bring to a boil. Cook until soft and ready to mash.

When done, strain potatoes and reserve cooking liquid. Mash the potatoes, using the reserved milk to bring to a creamy consistency. Add goat cheese, butter and sautéed leek. Season with truffle oil, salt and pepper.

Place the mashed potatoes on a large sheet of plastic and roll into a tube-like cylinder, approximately the size of a rolling pin. Refrigerate for 2 hours.

preparation. Preheat oven to 350°F. Wrap each filet with bacon and secure with butcher twine. Season with salt and pepper.

Remove the potato cylinder from the refrigerator and slice roll into 2-inch segments. Whisk eggs in small mixing bowl. Dip potato segments into egg, shaking off excess, then dip into panko, covering completely. Refrigerate for 30 minutes.

merlot demi-glace. While the potatoes are in the refrigerator, heat vegetable oil in heavy-bottomed sauce pot. Add meat scraps and brown well. Add shallot, garlic and bay leaf and cook until softened. Deglaze with red wine and reduce to ½ cup. Add stock. Strain through a fine sieve. Reduce until desired consistency is reached (approximately 35 to 45 minutes). It should be thick.

To finish the goat cheese tater tots, heat vegetable oil in sauté pan (fill about ½-inch deep), then deep fry both sides of potato segments until golden brown. Remove and place in the oven to keep warm.

Quickly sear or grill each side of the filet, then place in 350°F heated oven until medium rare, about 5 minutes. Remove from oven. Let rest.

Slice foie gras into four pieces and season with salt and pepper. Sear on high heat until cooked through.

final assembly and plating. Spoon demi-glace into tight circle on plate. Place each filet on the left with tater tots next to it on the right. Place foie gras on top of filet. Garnish with petite greens.

*For Snake River Farms Kobe beef filets, see sources on page 234.

 2006 Gemstone Estate Cabernet Sauvignon: Spicy and suave on the nose, the wine reveals opulence and layers of white chocolate, anise, licorice and black fruits.

Pistachio Cookies

Passion Fruit Soup

Chilled Passion Fruit Soup
with Vanilla Syrup, Pistachio Cookie and Coconut Gelato
serves 4

½ cup sugar

1 vanilla bean

¼ cup water

1 teaspoon cornstarch

1½ cups passion fruit juice
(at room temperature)

1 tablespoon white rum

2 tablespoons chilled butter,
cut into cubes

½ cup strawberries, diced

1 orange, segmented and
chopped

1 avocado, diced

3 basil leaves, roughly torn

Coconut Gelato

1 cup milk

1 can (14 ounces) cream of
coconut

1½ cups heavy cream

1½ cups sweetened flaked
coconut

Pistachio Cookies

1 cup butter, softened

½ cup shortening

1½ cups sugar

1 cup brown sugar

2 eggs

2 teaspoon vanilla extract

1½ cups all-purpose flour

1 cup whole wheat flour

½ cup rolled oats

1 teaspoon baking powder

1 teaspoon baking soda

1½ cups pistachio nuts,
chopped

coconut gelato. Prepare in advance. Combine milk and cream of coconut in food processor or blender, and mix thoroughly. Stir in cream and flaked coconut. Process in an ice cream maker according to manufacturer's instructions.

pistachio cookies. Makes 2 dozen cookies. Preheat oven to 350°F. In a large bowl, cream together butter, shortening, sugar and brown sugar until smooth. Beat in eggs one at a time, then stir in vanilla.
In a separate bowl, combine both flours, baking powder and baking soda.
Blend into creamed mixture to form dough. Fold in pistachios. Drop dough by teaspoonfuls onto ungreased cookie sheets.
Bake for 8 to 10 minutes. Allow cookies to cool on baking sheet for 5 minutes before removing to a wire rack to cool completely.

vanilla syrup. Cook water, sugar and vanilla bean in a separate saucepan until reduced to ¼ cup syrup, about 5 to 10 minutes. Thicken with cornstarch and set aside until ready to use.

preparation. Warm the passion fruit juice, rum and vanilla in a saucepan until slightly warm. Remove from heat. In a food processor, add the juice mixture and a cube of butter, one at a time, and blend until all are incorporated. (Use chilled butter, cold enough to be cut in cubes, but not too cold as this will prevent the soup from becoming oily, without hardening up.)

final assembly and plating. Place a pistachio cookie in the center of a low bowl and top with a large scoop of coconut ice cream. Slowly pour passion fruit soup around cookie and ice cream. Garnish with strawberries, oranges, avocado and basil. Serve immediately.

NOTE: Recipe requires ice cream maker.

2006 Gemstone Estate Cabernet Sauvignon: Spicy and suave on the nose, the wine reveals opulence and layers of flavors of white chocolate, anise, licorice and black fruits.

At the Nelson residence, bordered by wild sage and aspen trees, guests were treated to wines from Chappellet Vineyard, known for its innovative yet classic wines, and Villa Creek Cellars, famous for its complex, fruit-forward blends. Celebrated chef John Tesar created a mouth-watering menu to accompany the exquisite selections.

a selection of recipes from the
Nelson Residence
Hosted by Kipp Nelson
Chappellet Vineyard and Villa Creek Cellars
Chef John Tesar

starter
Sustainable Bigeye Tuna Foie Gras Tourchon
with Sea Salt and Riviera Ligure Olive Oil

2007 Villa Creek, Proprietary White

side
Pulled Braised Short Ribs
with Toasted Potato Gnocchi, Baby Peas and Wild Mushrooms

2005 Chappellet Pritchard Hill Cabernet Sauvignon

main
Herb and Garlic Crusted Rack of Veal

2006 Villa Creek, Willow Creek Cuvée

dessert
Poached Texas Peaches with Honey Bavarian Mousse,
Sable Breton and White Peach Sorbet

1998 Chappellet Liqueroux

Sustainable Bigeye Tuna Foie Gras Tourchon

Sustainable Bigeye Tuna Foie Gras Tourchon
with Sea Salt and Riviera Ligure Olive Oil
serves 6

1 pound sushi-grade
bigeye or yellowfin tuna

1 pound fresh duck foie gras
liver or finished terrine

2 bunches chives, minced

6 tablespoons extra
virgin olive oil (such as
Riviera de Liguria)

Maldon sea salt

Classic Terrine of Foie Gras

1 pound raw Grade A duck
foie gras at room temperature

4 teaspoons kosher salt

½ teaspoon freshly ground
white pepper

¼ cup Sauternes
(or 3 tablespoons Armagnac)

advance preparation. Remove all blood muscle or fiber from tuna. Slice cleaned fish into 2-ounce pieces (slicing the tuna thin or vertically). Place each piece in between 2 sheets of plastic wrap. Gently pound tuna into a paper thin circle. Once tuna is pounded, cut a 4-inch diameter circle out of cardboard, or using a ring mold cutter, trim pounded tuna into a perfect circle and refrigerate. Save cardboard circle to make the terrine of foie gras). Can be served with purchased foie gras terrine (available at specialty stores) or the adventurous cook can prepare it at home.

classic terrine of foie gras. Preheat oven to 200°F and line a small roasting pan with a folded kitchen towel or 6 layers of paper towels (this provides insulation so bottom of foie gras won't cook too quickly).
Sprinkle each lobe and any loose pieces of foie gras on both sides with kosher salt and white pepper. Sprinkle one third of Sauternes in terrine and firmly press large lobe of foie gras, smooth side down, into bottom. (Wedge any loose pieces of foie gras into terrine to make lobe fit snugly.) Sprinkle with another third of Sauternes. Put smaller lobe of foie gras, smooth side up, into terrine and firmly press down to create a flat surface and snug fit. Sprinkle with remaining Sauternes. Cover surface of foie gras with plastic wrap, then cover terrine with lid or foil.
Put terrine (with plastic wrap and lid) in roasting pan and fill roasting pan with enough hot water to reach halfway up side of terrine. Bake in the middle of oven until an instant-read thermometer inserted diagonally into center of foie gras registers 120°F, (1 to 1½ hours), or 160°F (for USDA standards; about 3½ hours). Remove terrine from pan. Discard water and remove towel. Return terrine to roasting pan and remove lid. Wrap the cardboard circle with plastic wrap and place directly on the surface of foie gras and set weight on cardboard (this will force fat to surface; don't worry if fat overflows). Let stand at room temperature 20 minutes. Remove weight and cardboard and spoon any fat that has dripped over side of terrine back onto top (fat will seal terrine). Chill, covered, until solid, at least 1 day.

final assembly and plating. Unmold foie gras by running a hot knife around edge. Invert onto a plate and reinvert, fat side up, onto serving dish. Cut into slices with a heated sharp knife. Take a chilled, round 10- to 11-inch plate and place 2 to 3 ounces of terrine (all fat removed) scattered around the interior of the plate in a 3- to 4-inch circle. Season with salt and cover with the pounded tuna removing the plastic wrap from one side and then flipping it over to cover terrine pieces and then removing the other piece of plastic so the tuna does not tear. Once in place, season with salt, cover with chopped chives and drizzle 1 tablespoon of extra virgin olive oil to finish.

2007 Villa Creek, Proprietary White:
A rich bouquet of white currants,
lemon blossoms and nectarines is
balanced by good acidity in this
fresh wine.

Pulled Braised Short Ribs

Pulled Braised Short Ribs
with Toasted Potato Gnocchi, Baby Peas and Wild Mushrooms
serves 8

2 tablespoons canola oil

6 short ribs with bones, cut 2 inches thick (about 4 pounds)

1 large onion, finely chopped

2 carrots, sliced

3 celery ribs, sliced

3 garlic cloves, thickly sliced

1 bottle dry red wine, such as Cabernet Sauvignon

4 thyme sprigs

3 cups chicken stock

salt and pepper to taste

½ cup peas, shelled (frozen peas can be used instead of fresh)

3 carrots, peeled, diced

2 cups braising liquid (from ribs), reduced

4 tablespoons sweet butter, softened

parmesan cheese, grated (for garnish)

Toasted Potato Gnocchi

(recipe and ingredients on next page)

advance preparation. Ribs can be made 1 to 2 days in advance (but must marinate overnight). Heat oil in a large sauté pan. Season ribs with salt and pepper. Add to the pan and cook over moderate heat, turning once, until browned and crusty (about 18 minutes). Transfer ribs in a single layer to a shallow baking dish.

Add the onion, carrots, celery and garlic to the pan and cook over low heat, stirring occasionally, until very soft and lightly browned (about 20 minutes). Add wine and thyme sprigs and bring to a boil over high heat. Pour hot marinade over ribs and let cool. Cover and refrigerate overnight, turning ribs once.

short ribs. Preheat the oven to 350°F. Transfer ribs and marinade to a large, enameled cast-iron casserole dish. Add chicken stock and bring to a boil. Cover and cook in the lower third of the oven for 1 hour 30 minutes, until meat is tender but not falling apart. Uncover and braise for 45 minutes longer, turning ribs once or twice, until sauce reduces by about half and meat is tender.

While meat is cooking, prepare the toasted potato gnocchi (recipe on next page). Once meat is cooked and sauce has been reduced by half, transfer meat to a clean shallow baking dish, discarding bones. Strain sauce into a heatproof measuring cup and skim off as much fat as possible. Pour sauce over meat (there should be about 2 cups). Let meat cool in liquid and then remove from pan until ready to use. Reserve liquid for the finished sauce.

Pull braised short ribs in the same manner as pulled pork or chicken or leave whole for a more hearty presentation. Set aside in a sauté pan in one tablespoon of butter. Slowly add blanched peas and carrots over a medium flame, roasting them in the foamy butter until golden brown. Once the vegetables turn golden, add pulled ribs and gently warm. When mixture is slightly warm, slowly add the reserved braising liquid, being careful not to boil the mixture.

Once the sauce has glazed the meat and vegetables, toast gnocchi (recipe on next page) in a heated Teflon pan with browned butter until golden brown. Once toasted, place on a paper towel to absorb any excess butter.

final assembly and plating. To plate, place 6 to 8 (or an even amount) of toasted gnocchi in a bowl. Spoon beef and vegetable mixture over top. Garnish with shavings of fresh parmesan cheese.

 2005 Chappellet Pritchard Hill Cabernet Sauvignon: Concentrated aromatics of black cherry, plum, dark chocolate, roast coffee and smoke segue to lush mouth-coating flavors of ripe berries, red currant, anise, vanilla, nutmeg and cedar.

Toasted Potato Gnocchi

Pulled Braised Short Ribs
with Toasted Potato Gnocchi, Baby Peas and Wild Mushrooms
(continued from page 193)

Toasted Potato Gnocchi

1 pound russet potatoes

3 to 4 egg yolks

½ cup freshly grated parmesan

¼ teaspoon freshly grated nutmeg

½ teaspoon salt

¼ teaspoon freshly ground black pepper

1 cup all-purpose flour, plus more for dusting board and dough

kosher salt

toasted potato gnocchi. Preheat oven to 425°F. Spread a layer of kosher salt on baking sheet and arrange potatoes on top. Bake until slightly overcooked, about 45 minutes. Let sit until cool enough to handle, cut in half, and scoop out the flesh. Reserve the potato skins, if desired, for another use.

Pass potatoes through a potato ricer or grate them on the large holes of a box grater. You should have about 2 cups. Make a mound of potatoes on the counter with a well in the middle; add 3 of the egg yolks, parmesan cheese, nutmeg, salt and pepper. Mix well with hands. Sprinkle ½ cup flour over the potatoes and, using your knuckles, press it into the potatoes. Fold over on itself and press down again. Sprinkle more flour, little by little, folding and pressing the dough until it just holds together (try not to knead it). Work any dough clinging to your fingers back into the dough. If the mixture is too dry, add another egg yolk or a little water. The dough should give under slight pressure. It will feel firm but yielding.

Keeping your work surface and the dough lightly floured, cut the dough into 4 pieces. Roll each piece into a rope about ½-inch in diameter. Cut each rope into ½-inch-long pieces, lightly flouring the gnocchi as you cut them. You can cook these as is or form them into the classic gnocchi shape with a gnocchi board, ridged butter paddle, or the tines of a large fork turned upside down. Rest the bottom edge of the gnocchi board on the work surface, then tilt it at about a 45-degree angle. Take each piece and squish it lightly with your thumb against the board while simultaneously pushing it away from you. It will roll away and around your thumb, taking on a cupped shape—with ridges on the outer curve from the board and a smooth surface on the inner curve where your thumb was. (Shaping them takes some time and dexterity. You might make a batch just for practice.) The indentation holds the sauce and helps gnocchi cook faster.

As you shape the gnocchi, dust them lightly with flour and scatter them on baking sheets lined with parchment paper or waxed paper. Set a gnocchi-filled cookie sheet in front of a fan on low for 30 minutes (turning gnocchi after 15 minutes). If you do not plan to cook the gnocchi until the next day or later, freeze them.

Herb and Garlic Crusted Rack of Veal

Herb and Garlic Crusted Rack of Veal
serves 2

2 veal chops (8 ounces), frenched

1 teaspoon olive oil

2 tablespoons Dijon mustard

8 cloves garlic

½ cup fresh breadcrumbs

¼ cup parmesan cheese

2 sprigs rosemary, chopped

¼ cup parsley, chopped

salt and pepper to taste

preparation. Preheat oven to 400°F and position oven rack in the middle. Season veal with salt and pepper. Heat a skillet over medium heat. Add olive oil and brown meat on all sides, about 3 minutes per side. Transfer meat to roasting pan and set aside to cool while you prepare the crust.

Purée Dijon mustard and garlic in a food processor. In a small bowl, stir together breadcrumbs, parmesan cheese, chopped rosemary and parsley. Season with salt and pepper to taste.

Rub browned meat with garlic and mustard mixture. Pat breadcrumb mixture into the mustard and garlic on the back or top of one side of the rack of veal, pressing slightly. Place unbreaded side down in a roasting pan. Roast veal until the internal temperature reads 125°F to 130°F, approximately 30 minutes to 1 hour. Remove veal from oven and let rest for 10 minutes.

final assembly and plating. Place a veal chop on each plate. Serving suggestion: garnish with potatoes roasted with garlic, rosemary butter and olive oil, salt and pepper, and/or a seasonal vegetable.

 2006 Villa Creek, Willow Creek Cuvée: Dark ruby in color with a nose of bacon, cherry cola, earth and meat. Nice combination of red and black fruits, spice, meat, coffee and cocoa on the palate.

Poached Texas Peaches

Poached Texas Peaches
with Honey Bavarian Mousse, Sable Breton and White Peach Sorbet
serves 12

6 peaches, halved and pitted

4 cups water

2 cups sugar

2 cups orange juice

1 vanilla bean

zest of one orange

1 sprig thyme

Honey Bavarian Mousse

1 cup cream

1 cup milk

¼ cup sugar

¼ cup honey

6 egg yolks

1 ounce pastry cream powder
(or 3 tablespoons cornstarch)

2½ teaspoons gelatin
(bloomed in 3 tablespoons
cold water)

1 cup cream (whipped into
soft peaks)

White Peach Sorbet

(recipe and ingredients
on next page)

Sable Breton

(recipe and ingredients
on next page)

advance preparation. Prepare the white peach sorbet (recipe on next page) at least one day in advance.

preparation. Prepare the sable breton cookies (recipe on next page), then the honey bavarian mousse.

honey bavarian mousse. Bloom gelatin by sprinkling the gelatin evenly over the 3 tablespoons of cold water and let sit for 4 to 5 minutes ("blooming" the gelatin, scattering it evenly over the surface of the cold water, prevents it from forming in clumps and ensures a smooth texture, so that when the gelatin is heated, it will dissolve evenly).
Combine milk and 1 cup of cream in a sauce pan and bring to a simmer. Whisk sugar, pastry cream powder (or cornstarch) and honey into the yolks. Temper warm liquid into yolk mixture to prevent the eggs from scrambling. Return mixture to heat and bring to a boil, whisking regularly.
Remove from heat and add bloomed gelatin. Place in a bowl, cover top with plastic wrap placed directly on the surface of the cream, and let cool.
Once cooled, fold in whipped cream and pour into decorative 4-ounce mold or individual ramekins and chill for 1 hour.

poached texas peaches. While honey bavarian mousse is allowed to set, split peaches and remove pit. Place water, sugar, orange juice, vanilla bean, orange zest and thyme sprig in a sauce pan, then add peaches. Bring to a rapid simmer, then remove from heat. Let cool slightly, remove peaches (reserving juice mixture) and peel while warm. Set peaches aside for final plating.
Put reserved peach juice mixture (minus peaches) back on the stove and simmer until reduced by half. Remove vanilla bean and thyme sprig.

final assembly and plating. Remove honey bavarian mousse from mold. Dip mold briefly in hot water and shake gently onto serving platter. Arrange grilled fruit pieces on a plate, drizzle with reduced peach juice mixture and top with a scoop of white peach sorbet.

 1998 Chappellet Liqueroux: Intense aromas of ripe peaches and baked pineapple are accented with notes of citrus marmalade and oak spice. Nutmeg and clove flavors add to the complexity.

Sable Breton Cookies

White Peach Sorbet

Poached Texas Peaches
with Honey Bavarian Mousse, Sable Breton and White Peach Sorbet
(continued from page 199)

White Peach Sorbet

4½ cups peach purée

2 cups water

1⅓ cups sugar

7 tablespoons glucose powder
(can substitute corn syrup)

Sable Breton Cookies

(makes approximately
2 dozen cookies)

5 egg yolks

¾ cup, plus 2 tablespoons
sugar

12 tablespoons butter
(at room temperature)

½ cup, plus 1 tablespoon
all-purpose flour

½ cup, plus 1 tablespoon
cake flour

4 teaspoons baking powder

white peach sorbet. Combine peach purée, water, sugar and glucose powder (or corn syrup) in the bowl of a residential ice cream maker and prepare according to manufacturer's instructions. Freeze.

sable breton cookies. In a stand-up mixer with whisk attachment, whip yolks and sugar to ribbon stage (the ribbon stage is reached when the whisk leaves a trail behind that is visible for a short while before merging back into the mixture; you should be able to see the bottom of the bowl for a split second before it fills back in). The purpose of blending until ribbon stage is to incorporate some air into the mixture, and also to ensure that the sugar is thoroughly dissolved so that the egg mixture does not become granular when heated later.
Slowly add butter in small pieces to the yolk mixture.
In a separate bowl, combine both flours, baking powder and salt. Add to the yolk mixture, combining ingredients in mixer. Be careful not to over mix.
Transfer dough to a lightly-floured work surface and press into a disc. Wrap in plastic wrap and refrigerate until chilled, about 1 hour.
Preheat oven to 350°F.
On a lightly-floured surface, roll out dough to ¼-inch thick or more. Cut out rounds using a 3-inch fluted cookie cutter. Place rounds on baking sheet with parchment paper or silicone non-stick baking mat. Bake in center rack until lightly golden, about 12 to 15 minutes.
Transfer cookies to rack and cool.

style tips

Floral arrangements can be inventive and unique by adding unexpected elements—cinnamon sticks as a backdrop for orchids, cabbages as flowers or fragrant branches and vines.

cinnamon stick collage

An unusual centerpiece for a casual dinner party, this rustic arrangement combines everyday cinnamon with beautiful orchids and loose greens. The arrangement is simple and easily constructed, but also offers a modern look. (florals used: White Phalaenopsis blooms and hanging Amaranthus). *Courtesy Sue Bridgman Florist.*

cabbage décor

Looking for something out of the ordinary?
Combine flowers with food elements like cabbage
or kale. Display in a cluster setting on your buffet
table or line them up on your dining table. The
goal is to create a modern arrangement, using food
and florals (cabbage, kale, lime carnations, green
Tricillium, Ornithogalum florettes, and Berzillia
berries). *Courtesy Sue Bridgman Florist.*

branches and vines

Branches and vines can be fragrant and long-
lasting. Just remember to change water on all
flower arrangements every three days. On taller
arrangements, refresh the water by placing the vase
in the sink, putting the water hose into the side of
the arrangement and allowing it to rinse through for
a few minutes. *Courtesy Taylor'd Events.*

The food and wines presented at the Vogels' unique home exemplified elegance and balance. The Booker Vineyard wine selections showcased superb fruit purity and full-bodied power, while Trefethen Family Vineyards' signature varietals were full of sheer intensity, matched only by their refinement. Taite Pearson of SEGO Restaurant & Bar astonished the palate with contemporary, sustainable American cuisine.

a selection of recipes from the

Vogel Residence

Hosted by Jill and Fred Vogel and Wells Fargo, The Private Bank
Booker Vineyard and Trefethen Family Vineyards
Chef Taite Pearson and Pastry Chef Sarah Lipton

starter
Braised Leg of Rabbit with Sausage, Garganelli
and Red Wine Marinated Huckleberries

2008 Booker "Fracture" Syrah

main
Braised Pork Cheeks and Confit Belly with
Cauliflower Purée, Romanesco and Chanterelles

2005 Trefethen Cabernet Sauvignon

dessert
Olive Oil Cake with Red Wine Plums
and Pluot Sorbet

2008 Booker "The Ripper" Grenache

trefethen, booker, and sego

the food

passed foie gras / figs and duck prosciutto / melon
idaho caviar corn pudding, brioche, quail egg
golden trout fennel, mustard, tomato
confit rabbit sausage, hand rolled pasta, black raspberries
pork cheek and belly chanterelles, romanesco, bordelaise
olive oil cake red wine plums, pluot sorbet

the wine

2006 **trefethen** dry riesling
2008 **booker** "white" roussane/viognier
2007 **trefethen** chardonnay
2008 **booker** "fracture" syrah
2005 **trefethen** cabernet sauvignon
2008 **booker** "the ripper" grenache

the farmers, ranchers and artisans

ca bull elk ranch	springs of life
golden premier farm	cloverleaf creamery
purple sage farm	fair mountain farm
rice family farms	fish processors of idaho
rolling stone chevre	gem farms
snake river farms	niman ranch
vee bee honey	springs ranch
zursun beans	sweet valley organics

the hosts

wells fargo / jill and fred vogel

Braised Leg of Rabbit

Braised Leg of Rabbit
with Sausage, Garganelli and Red Wine Marinated Huckleberries
serves 4

1 package garganelli pasta
(about 48 pieces)

2 cups rabbit jus
(from braising)

4 cups tuscan kale
(approximately 1 bunch),
cleaned and chopped

2 shallots, sliced thin

4 tablespoons red wine
marinated huckleberries
(recipe below)

1 tablespoon butter

2 tablespoons olive oil

salt and pepper to taste

Rabbit Sausage

8 ounces rabbit loin,
cut into 1-inch pieces

8 ounces pork shoulder,
cut into 1-inch pieces

4 garlic cloves, chopped

½ cup olive oil

½ cup chopped parsley

2 tablespoons champagne
vinegar

1 teaspoon ground mace

1 teaspoon fresh ground
black pepper

2 teaspoons salt

½ teaspoon pink curing salt

Braised Leg of Rabbit

(recipe and ingredients
on next page)

Red Wine Marinated
Huckleberries

(recipe and ingredients
on next page)

advance preparation. Prepare rabbit sausage (recipe below) and braised rabbit legs (recipe on next page) and refrigerate. Both can be made one day ahead.

rabbit sausage. Yields about 10 sausages. Mix all ingredients together and place in freezer for 1 hour.
Set up meat grinder with ³⁄₁₆-inch plate. Pass all ingredients through grinder into a mixing bowl. Mix vigorously in circular motions, by hand, to assure a smooth emulsification. Case farce into hog casings, tying off or twisting to form 3-inch sausages. Refrigerate until ready to use. Can be made ahead and refrigerated.

preparation. Prepare red wine marinated huckleberries (recipe on next page). Preheat oven to 375°F. Fill a medium pot with water. Salt and bring to a boil.
Wash and dry the kale, and set aside (if using another varietal other than Tuscan kale, parboil briefly and set aside for final sauté step).
Place finished braised rabbit legs and reserved jus (prepared in advance, recipe on next page) in a small sauce pot and bring to a simmer.
Heat a medium sauté pan to medium heat. Add rabbit sausages to pan and cook, rolling as they brown. Once evenly colored, put pan in oven for 6 minutes, then remove pan from oven and place back on burner on high heat. Add olive oil and shallots to pan and caramelize lightly, then add kale and jus from rabbit leg pot. Season with salt and pepper and cook until kale is soft and liquid is reduced to almost none.
Drop the garganelli pasta in the pot of boiling water and cook until done (al dente). Strain pasta, then add pasta and butter to the sauté pan with the sausages, shallots and kale.
Remove sausages from pan to a cutting board and cut in half lengthwise. Set aside for plating. Check seasonings again and adjust if necessary.

final assembly and plating. Plate in four wide-bottom bowls. Divide pasta and kale equally, spooning extra jus into bowls. Place one leg and two halves of sausage in each bowl and spoon a tablespoon of huckleberries, in small dollops, into each bowl.

2008 Booker "Fracture" Syrah:
Boasting a massive mid-palate and a long fruit-driven finish, this wine's light smoky notes and hints of chocolate also shine through.

Red Wine Marinated Huckleberries

Braised Leg of Rabbit
with Sausage, Garganelli and Red Wine Marinated Huckleberries
(continued from page 207)

Braised Leg of Rabbit

4 rabbit legs

2 celery sticks

1 medium carrot, peeled and split down middle

1 medium white onion, peeled and cut in half

4 garlic cloves

¼ cup golden raisins

4 thyme sprigs

2 bay leaves

½ cup Madeira

1½ cup white wine, Chardonnay preferred

1 quart chicken stock

¼ cup grapeseed or neutral oil

salt and pepper to taste

Red Wine Marinated Huckleberries

1 cup huckleberries

1 cup red wine, Pinot Noir preferred

1 cinnamon stick

1 teaspoon juniper berries

4 tablespoons honey

1 tablespoon orange zest

½ teaspoon cracked black peppercorns

braised leg of rabbit. Heat a medium sauce pot to medium heat. Season rabbit legs generously with salt and pepper. Add oil to pot and sear legs on all sides to a golden brown. Add carrots, celery and onion, and brown. Add garlic, raisins, thyme and bay leaves and cook until fragrant. Deglaze with Madeira. Add white wine and reduce by half.
Add chicken stock. Bring to a soft boil. Remove from heat, cover and transfer to preheated oven. Cook for 3 hours or until meat barely holds to bone. Cool and store in liquid until ready to use, reserving jus to use later in finished sauce.

red wine marinated huckleberries. Place huckleberries in a small bowl and set aside. In a small sauce pot, add red wine, cinnamon, juniper berries, honey, orange zest and cracked black peppercorns and bring to a boil. Reduce volume by ¼. Pour the reduced sauce over the huckleberries and allow to marinate for at least one hour before serving.

Braised Pork Cheeks and Confit Belly

Braised Pork Cheeks and Confit Belly
with Cauliflower Purée, Romanesco and Chanterelles
serves 4

1 cup romanesco,
cut into ½ inch florets

1 cup chanterelle mushrooms,
stems trimmed and peeled

1 teaspoon fresh thyme
leaves

2 tablespoon butter

1 tablespoon grapeseed
or neutral oil

sea salt and freshly ground
pepper to taste

Confit Pork Belly

1½ pounds pork belly

½ cup kosher salt

¼ cup sugar

1 tablespoon pink curing salt

1 tablespoon black
peppercorns, crushed coarse

1 teaspoon coriander seeds,
crushed coarse

1½ quart rendered duck fat

Cauliflower Purée

(recipe and ingredients
on next page)

Red Wine Braised
Pork Cheeks

(recipe and ingredients
on next page)

advance preparation. Prepare the red wine braised pork cheeks several days in advance (recipe follows on next page). Prepare the confit pork belly at least one day in advance.

confit pork belly. Mix together salt, sugar and curing salt. Rub entire pork belly evenly with salt mixture and refrigerate, covered, for 24 hours.
After 24 hours, preheat oven to 225°F. Crust the top, or fattiest side, of the belly with the pepper and crushed coriander seeds. Place belly in a casserole-style dish not much bigger than the belly and twice as high and set aside.
Heat the duck fat until barely melted. Pour fat over pork belly and cover dish with foil. Place in preheated oven and cook for 4 hours at 225°F or until entire belly is gelatinous in texture. Remove foil and cool in refrigerator in cooking vessel. Once cool, remove belly from fat and cut into 2 x 2 x 2-inch cubes and set aside until ready to finish the dish.

preparation. Place cheeks in a large sauté pan with half of braising liquid and turn heat to medium.
Heat a small sauté pan to medium heat and add cubes of pork belly, fattiest side down. After pork cheeks come to a simmer, begin basting cheeks with braising liquid. Do this continuously.
Once pork belly has become golden and crisp on the first side, turn pan to low heat and turn cube to another side. Continue turning cubes to each side until all are crisp and golden, basting with braising liquid continuously. Once all sides are done, place pork belly on paper towel on a plate and keep warm.
Meanwhile, reduce remaining pork cheek liquid in large sauté pan, while basting, until it reaches a glaze consistency. Cover and set aside, keeping warm until ready to plate. Heat a medium sauté pan to medium-high heat and add oil. Place romanesco in pan and sauté until slightly caramelized. Add chanterelles and butter, season to taste with salt and pepper and continue sautéing until mushrooms get a bit of color. Add thyme and remove from heat, keeping warm until plating. Prepare the cauliflower purée (recipe follows on next page).

final assembly and plating. Set out four large dinner plates. Spoon equal amounts of cauliflower purée into the middle of each plate. Spread into a smooth oval. Place two cheeks in the middle of purée on each plate, spooning reduced braising liquid over cheeks. Place confit pork belly cubes next to cheeks and arrange equal amounts of romanesco and chanterelles on and around cheeks. Serve immediately.

NOTE: Native to Italy, Romanesco is also known as Romanesco broccoli or Roman cauliflower. It is available in specialty markets and should not be confused with Broccoflower (which is a green cauliflower).

2005 Trefethen Cabernet Sauvignon:
Deep ruby in color, this complex wine exhibits a luxurious nose of blackberry, black cherry, plum, black currant, black pepper, cola nut and chocolate with a hint of black pepper and olive.

Cauliflower Purée

Red Wine Braised Pork Cheeks

Braised Pork Cheeks and Confit Belly
with Cauliflower Purée, Romanesco and Chanterelles
(continued from page 211)

Cauliflower Purée

1 cauliflower, cut into
½ inch florets

2 cups whole milk

1 teaspoon kosher salt

¼ teaspoon fresh ground
white pepper

4 tablespoons butter

Red Wine Braised
Pork Cheeks

8 pork cheeks

1 large carrot, peeled and
cut in half lengthwise

2 celery stalks, cut into
5-inch pieces

1 large yellow onion, peeled
and cut in half

5 garlic cloves, smashed

5 sprigs thyme

8 parsley stems

3 bay leaves

½ bottle (375ml) Cabernet
Sauvignon

½ cup soy sauce

¼ cup pomegranate molasses*

6 cups chicken stock

¼ cup neutral oil,
grapeseed preferred

salt and pepper to taste

cauliflower purée. Place cauliflower, milk, salt and pepper in a small sauce pot. Cook over low heat, covered, until cauliflower is soft. Strain off and discard milk. Transfer cauliflower to high-speed blender. Add butter and blend until smooth. Adjust seasoning, if necessary. Hold warm in small sauce pot until final assembly and plating.

red wine braised pork cheeks. Preheat oven to 240°F.
Heat a medium sauce pot to very hot. Add oil and sear cheeks, taking care to get a nice golden brown on all sides. Remove cheeks. Dump any residual oil, then caramelize carrot, celery and onion in same pot. Add cheeks back to pot and deglaze with wine and soy sauce. Bring to simmer and reduce liquid by half. Once reduced, add garlic, herbs, pomegranate molasses and stock and bring to a gentle simmer. Cover pot with lid or foil and place in oven for 4 hours.
After 4 hours, remove from oven. Remove cheeks from liquid and place in an additional pot. Strain liquid through a fine mesh strainer and pour over cheeks. Set cheeks aside, keeping warm, if using right away. This should yield 4 portions, or 8 cheeks. You can braise these up to a few days in advance and refrigerate until ready to use.

*For pomegranate molasses, see sources on page 234.

Olive Oil Cake

Olive Oil Cake
with Red Wine Plums and Pluot Sorbet
serves 8

2⅓ cups sugar

3 whole eggs

1 egg yolk

1 lemon, zested and juiced (optional)

1 teaspoon kosher salt

1¾ cups olive oil

1½ cups orange juice, fresh squeezed

1½ cups whole milk

2⅓ cups all purpose flour, sifted

¾ teaspoon baking soda, sifted with flour

¾ teaspoon baking powder, sifted with flour

Pluot Sorbet

4½ cups pluots*, pits removed and roughly chopped (measure after pits removed)

1 cup sugar

1 cup water

½ lemon, juiced

Red Wine Plums

6 plums, halved and pitted

1 (750ml) bottle red wine

6 cardamon pods

1 vanilla bean, split and scraped

1 cinnamon stick

4 cloves

4 black peppercorns

¾ cup sugar

¼ cup brown sugar

1 orange, zest strips only

½ cup water

advance preparation. Preheat oven to 350°F. In a small bowl, combine sifted flour, baking soda and baking powder and set aside.
Combine sugar and eggs in mixer and whip until ribbon stage. Add lemon zest, juice and salt. Slowly mix in olive oil, orange juice and milk. Fold in sifted dry ingredients. Pour into a parchment-lined 9 x 13-inch pan. Using a convection oven (or convection setting) bake at 350°F on high fan for 15 minutes, then turn fan to low and bake completely prior to removing from pan (if no convection setting, bake at 350°F until done). It's best to leave pan overnight in refrigerator.

pluot sorbet. Combine 1 cup sugar and 1 cup water in saucepan and bring to a boil to create a simple syrup. Allow to cool to room temperature.
When cool, combine simple syrup, pluots (plum and apricot hybrid) and lemon juice in a blender. Blend until smooth. Pour into ice cream machine and process according to manufacturer's instructions. Store in freezer until ready to use. Allow to temper for 2 to 3 minutes prior to scooping.

red wine plums. Combine plums, red wine, cardamon pods, vanilla bean, cinnamon stick, cloves, peppercorns, sugar, brown sugar, orange zest and water in a pot small enough so the liquid covers the plums when combined. Bring to a simmer. Allow to simmer until plums are almost fork-tender. Remove 8 plum halves and allow to cool. Leave remaining plums and liquid on stove and reduce by ¼. Strain and reserve sauce. Store the sauce and plums separately, or serve immediately. To serve, heat plums and sauce together, serve plums with sauce spooned over top.

final assembly and plating. Cut the olive oil cake to desired size and bring to room temperature prior to plating. Cut cake when cold and use a serrated knife; it will be easier to slice. This recipe calls for the cake at room temperature, however, it can also be served warm if desired.
Bring poached plums to room temperature and heat the sauce to barely a simmer. Place the cake in the middle of the plate, put one half of a plum on top of the cake and another half of the plum leaning against the cake. Spoon 3 tablespoons of sauce over the top of the plums. Scoop the pluot sorbet and place on top.

NOTE: Recipe requires an ice cream maker.

*Pluots are a type of plum and apricot hybrid available at farmer's markets and specialty produce stores.

 2008 Booker "The Ripper" Grenache: Strawberry and dark cherry flavors show themselves right away. The wine's full body lingers on the palate while presenting stunning opulence, purity and length.

all about wine

A resource guide for the wine connoisseur: all about tasting, storing, bottles, grape varieties and vintages. Use the following tips and tools to plan your wine party or dinner and select the perfect varietal for any meal.

taste is everything

Eat, drink and be merry. The proposition seems simple enough. But when pairing food and wine, it can take a turn towards the perplexing. Fortunately, training the palate and preparing for future dinner party success and wine selection brilliance is as simple as following the same adage: Eat, drink and be merry!

drink what you love. Drinking wine is a singular experience. Everyone's palate is different. Follow your taste, and don't be swayed by siren songs of the highly rated, popular or prestigious. Only you know what you love. So drink and explore the types of wine that speak to you, at whatever price works for your budget, and enjoy every sip along the way.

sample and savor. Green apple. Red plum. Blackberry. Tobacco. Chocolate. Black pepper. Wine transforms the mere grape into a field of flavors—distinctive notes that speak to the complexities and nuances of various grape varietals, appellations, growing seasons, vineyards and vintners. Tasting this distinction between different varietals can be the difficult part. A wine tasting party gives people a chance to make the glass in front of them the center of attention. The conversations and comparisons that ensue broaden everyone's understanding of the way different wines react on palates and to food.

theme party. Random selection is not always the best way to advance a wine tasting party. Instead, choose a theme and invite each taster to bring a bottle that relates to it. Theme tastings can bring out the subtleties between wines of the same region, varietal, vintage or another distinction.

wine tasting ideas

vertical tasting. A comparison of different vintages of the same wine.

horizontal tasting. A comparison of different wines of the same vintner.

comparative tasting. A comparison of different examples of the same style of wine.

blind tasting. Identify and rate unmarked wines.

terms

punt. The indentation in the bottom of the wine bottle.

must. The fermenting juice; the halfway stage between grape juice and wine.

amelioration. The official term used to cover cellar practices which include the adding of sugar, the "correcting" of the wine's acidity, the addition of water to reduce acidity or to compensate for overripe grapes. Some of the practices are necessary, while others can be illegal.

aroma. A wine's aroma is most distinctive when the wine is young because it is directly related to the odor of fresh fruit.

bouquet. A wine's bouquet is different than its aroma. The bouquet is the smell, or combination of smells, that evolves with time as the wine ages in the bottle.

France consumes more wine than any other country (12.4% of world wine consumption in 2009). However, in per capita wine consumption the Vatican City State, at 70 liters per capita, Luxembourg and Norfolk Island beat France, which only consumes 45 liters per capita.

how to taste

Rarely do we make the time to truly focus on the taste of our wine. Incorporating a quick evaluation into an everyday wine experience will reward you exponentially in understanding and enjoyment.

Above all else, start fresh with each glass. Focus. If you like, clear your palate with water, plain bread or a cracker. When tasting, take note of three simple senses in the order shown below. Use the tasting notes example as a reference to take your own notes at your next tasting party.

sight. Looks say so much about the strength of a wine. A pale, translucent wine will likely be light and delicate in its aroma, flavor and feel in the mouth. Deep gold in a white wine or opaque purple in a red indicate a more powerful flavor profile.

smell. Before you taste, smell. Fill your glass no more than to where the bowl starts to narrow—the golden rule being never fill past the widest part. Holding the glass by the stem, swirl the wine. Tilt the glass towards you and—with your nose inside the bowl—take a deep sniff. Wines can express hundreds of aromas as bouquet, but don't worry. Think about categories, rather than specific smells. Distinguish between floral, fruit, herbal and spice notes.

taste. Finally, it's time for the concluding sensation: taste. Take a sip of wine, enough to coat the tongue. Purse your lips and draw air in to release the wine's volatile compounds. Roll the wine around in your mouth. Think about the flavors, texture and how it feels. The tongue registers numerous flavors but there are three basics when it comes to wine: sweetness at the front of the tongue, sourness or acidity at the sides, and bitterness at the back. Take note of the levels of all three. This will serve you greatly when later pairing food and wine.

flavor categories

1. Riesling/ Sauvignon Blanc
Think Green: green apple and pear, kiwi, lime and grass.

2. Chardonnay
Think Yellow: yellow plum and tomato, lemon, butter, butterscotch and vanilla.

3. Pinot Noir, Sangiovese
Think Red: red plum, berry and cherry, baking spices and earth.

4. Merlot
Think Purple: dark plum and dark cherry.

5. Syrah, Cabernet Sauvignon
Think Black: blackberry, blackcurrant, fig, meat, pepper, coffee and black licorice.

matching food with wine. As in love, ideal pairings of food and wine take synchronicity. Sometimes, the flavors complement each other. At other times, they contrast but never clash. And in certain magical instances, they do both—complement and contrast—at once.

basic wine characteristics. Hundreds of flavors reside in wine, but as a starting place, think in terms of categories of flavor. Use the notes (bottom left) to find basic taste distinctions across the flavor spectrum of wine.

tasting notes

Create note cards for your own tasting party using the categories below for guest comment and rating.

1. Wine Name

2. Color and Intensity
Color: pale yellow, yellow-green, gold, ruby, red, deep purple, garnet
Saturation: high or low

3. Aroma or Bouquet
Note the initial smell or nose of the wine. The flavor on your palate may be different than the initial aroma or bouquet. Strong or mild: apple, pear, peach, lemon, mango, blueberry, black currant, strawberry, cherry, fig, melon, tropical fruits, raisin, tart, sweet, herbal, grass, green pepper, caramel, vanilla, honey, smoky, pepper, tobacco, leather, mineral, earth.

4. Flavors, Acidity, Sweetness and Balance
Flavor taste profiles are classified generally as sweet, sour, salty, bitter or pungent
Acidity: high or low
Sweetness: high or low
Balance

5. Tannins, Body and Alcohol
Tannins: high or low
Body/Texture: thick or thin
Alcohol level: high or low

6. Finish and Complexity
Finish: long or short
Complexity: multidimensional or straightforward

grapes and varietals

Over 10,000 grape varieties exist, but wine producers draw on only about 50 or so for wide-scale wine production. Grapes are at the essence of every wine, and its final aroma, color and character largely depend on the original varietal used.

A varietal indicates a wine made primarily from a single grape variety—at least 75% of the wine must come from the specific grape varietal for it to carry that name—such as Chardonnay, Merlot or Cabernet Sauvignon. The appellation (the terroir, which is the special character and flavor that geography, soil and climate bestow upon a grape), the treatment of the vineyards (how planted, cared for and harvested) and the techniques and experience of the individual winemaker are also important factors.

As a way to provide a basic outline of typical flavor and aroma profiles of the more popular varietals, the most recognizable are broken down below by classic white and classic red grapes. Wine lovers should note, however, that many other important varieties exist that deserve mention and are worth exploration (such as Sémillon, Chenin Blanc, Trebbiano, Silvaner, Müller-Thurgau, and Pinot Blanc in the family of white grapes; and Cabernet Franc, Gamay, Cinsault, Carignan, Carmenère, Malbec, Mourvèdre, Petit Verdot, Barbera, Nebbiolo, Sangiovese and Tempranillo in the red grape family). The beauty of winemaking is that new clones are created to improve upon a particular flavor profile and older cultivars are often "rediscovered" and appreciated for their own merit, so exploring often adds to the enjoyment of new wine varietals.

Classic White Grapes

chardonnay. The grape grown around the world, Chardonnay can be successful in both cool and warm climates. As a varietal, Chardonnay is often perceived as a wine that "tastes like oak." But Chardonnay grapes impart numerous flavors, especially refreshing acidic apple and citrus notes that run anywhere from light, crisp and green, to rich and sweet tropical notes. Oak is often added to the equation with the use of oak barrels or chips included during aging, causing the wine to take on vanilla or buttered-toast flavors.

gewurztraminer. Spices, honeysuckle or rose petals are all flavors that can come from a grape that's surprisingly easy to pronounce: Gewurztraminer (guh-VERTZ-tra-mee-ner). Like the name, this varietal is bold, voluptuous and exotic. Exemplary Gewurztraminer vineyards lie in cool-weather regions and produce low yields. Classic Gewurztraminers from the Old World are dry, with forward flavors of heady fruit and allspice, clove and cardamom. New World Gewurztraminers range in style and tend to be known for sweetness and perfume.

pinot grigio/pinot gris. Pinot Gris, prominently found in Alsace, France, produces wines laden with spice, honey and tropical flavors—perfumed, aromatic and typically dry. Pinot Grigio, a slight variation of the grape from Italy, creates a crisp, high acid, citrus-noted wine. Pinot Gris/Pinot Grigio varies widely depending on the vineyard, and often plays the role of simply not offending food, rather than enhancing it. Oregon and California are also known for producing this varietal.

riesling. A misunderstood varietal. Many people think Rieslings are sweet wines that need to be served with sweet food. Not quite. The Riesling grape can make extraordinary wines across the palate, from bone-dry to achingly sweet. Riesling wine originated in Germany's Rhein and Mosel river valleys. It is a sensitive varietal, requiring specific climate (cold) and soil conditions (solid, quick draining) to thrive. The flavor profile of the wine varies dramatically with the vineyard and growing region. High acid is a hallmark, with notes of citrus and fruits.

sauvignon blanc. Think green. Sauvignon Blanc is gaining in popularity by showcasing a spectrum of flavors and aromas that center on green—from green apples and grapes, to herbs, lime, kiwi, honeydew melon, guava, papaya, and passion fruit. Sauvignon Blanc makes both subtle and dramatic shifts on the flavor scale depending on where the grapes are grown.

viognier. Surprisingly easy to drink, but not as easy to pronounce, Viognier (vee-own-YAY) is closely identified with the northern Rhône Valley in France. But this varietal has made a sizeable footprint in the warm climates of the New World. Viogniers impart several layers of aroma and complexities, sharing the tropical fruit flavors and creamy mouthfeel of a Chardonnay, and echoing the sweet, distinctive profile of a Gewurztraminer. Viogniers often get paired with the same foods as Chardonnay, with the added benefit of enhancing, not overwhelming, most flavors.

California is America's top wine producer, making 90% of all U.S. wine exports and over 197 million cases within the United States in 2009. Chardonnay, Cabernet Sauvignon and Zinfandel are currently the top three varieties.

Classic Red Grapes

cabernet sauvignon. Regions that are moderately warm to hot make happy homes for Cabernet Sauvignon, and this varietal is certainly hot in the marketplace. Cabernet Sauvignon is known and well-loved for offering vibrant aromas of black cherries, currants, black plums, with traces of black olives in a young wine, and hints of cedar and cigar in aged bottles. Cabs, as they're often simply called, offer a reliable, full-bodied appeal, with high degrees of tannins and acidity.

grenache. Grenache is the most widely planted red grape in the world, primarily in Spain, where it is called "Garnacha." Grenache is high in sugars, and therefore achieves higher alcohol content. Often used as a blend, this varietal is gaining ground as a stand-alone wine with fruity flavors and dashes of herbal notes that compare favorably to Pinot Noir.

merlot. With rich, sweet flavors and low levels of tannins and acidity, Merlot was long viewed more as a blender than a stand-alone varietal. But this varietal began to be noticed in the 1980s, and has continued to grow in popularity since. Some say Merlot lacks a "middle palate," the lasting weight and presence of the wine after the first encounter with the tongue and mouth. But others enjoy it for its sweet start and smooth finish. Merlot takes on several styles, but usually poses little challenge to the palate or food pairings.

pinot noir. Pinot Noir is a sensitive, finicky grape that is difficult to grow but very rewarding to drink. By law in France, Pinot Noir is the only red grape grown in the best vineyard sites in Burgundy. The character of different Pinot Noirs comes down to the uniqueness of individual vineyards and vintners. Each Pinot Noir seduces in different ways. Its flavors sing of sweet red berries, plums, tomatoes, cherries and, at times, a notable earthy or wood-like flavor. Pinot Noir is considered to be the most food-friendly red wine. It pairs well with poultry, beef, fish, ham, lamb and pork, and complements creamy sauces and spicy seasonings.

syrah/shiraz. Syrah and Shiraz are the same grape with different monikers depending on where they are grown. Syrah is grown in Europe and many parts of America. Shiraz is more often identified with Australia, where it is the most popular grape variety produced. Many different styles of Syrah/Shiraz exist, and the wine is not easy to pin down. It can be light- to medium-bodied or full and rich, with firm tannins and strong flavors of black cherry, blackberry, plum, bell pepper, black pepper, clove, licorice, dark chocolate or smoked meat.

zinfandel. While factions from California to Italy and Croatia debate the true origin of this grape, there's no debate that Zinfandel has become increasingly popular with consumers. This heat-loving varietal is a deep red, almost black grape. Pink and white versions of Zinfandel simply have little to no contact with the skins of the grape. Look for the aroma of fruits like raspberries, cranberries and strawberries in light versions, and black cherries, black plums, or raisins and figs, in the big-bodied variations.

how to store wine

The best temperature to store wine is anywhere from 40°F to 60°F depending on the varietal. However, some people believe that 52°F is an ideal temperature for all varieties.

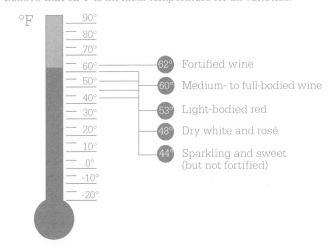

62° Fortified wine

60° Medium- to full-bodied wine

53° Light-bodied red

48° Dry white and rosé

44° Sparkling and sweet (but not fortified)

unique wine facts

- The former French colony of Algeria (now an independent country on the Mediterranean coast of North Africa) has over 800,000 acres of vineyards planted by French settlers about 100 years ago.

- From 1920 to 1933, during Prohibition when the production and sale of wine was restricted to religious and medical purposes, the planting and growing of grapes actually accelerated, resulting in a dramatic doubling of vineyards.

- The most expensive bottle of wine ever sold at auction went for approximately $150,000. It was a bottle of 1787 Château Lafite that had been owned by Thomas Jefferson. It was a standard size bottle and was purchased by the Forbes (magazine) family.

- There are approximately 1,000 named vineyards in Bordeaux.

- The approximate annual wine production from the village of Blaye in Bordeaux is 4 million gallons. The entire Bordeaux region produces 85 million gallons of wine each year.

- The Beringer Winery in Napa Valley alone produces more Chardonnay than the entire district of Chablis in Burgundy, France, the grape's most famous home.

- Chile is the oldest wine-producing country in South America.

- Blanc de Blancs refers to a white wine or Champagne made from white-skinned grapes, while Blanc de Noirs refers to a white wine made from black (purple or red) grapes.

- The earliest literary references to wine were found in picture writings of the ancient Egyptians and Babylonians, about 5,000 years ago.

- A hectare is equal to 2.471 acres.

- Vitis Vinifera is the grape species that was brought north by the Romans, who received it earlier from ancient Persia and Greece. This species exists now in every winemaking country and produces 98% of the world's wine.

SOURCE: Thornton, Jack W. So You Think you Know Wine. Boston: Quinlan Press, 1989.

Australia is best known for Shiraz (the same grape as Syrah), which has typically been the most-produced variety, followed by Cabernet Sauvignon, Chardonnay, Sémillon and Sauvignon Blanc.

how to read a wine label

Deciphering labels can be tricky business—since each country is governed by different rules and regulations about what must be printed on the wine label. In the U.S., for example, many wines are named for the variety of grape from which they are produced, so it appears on the label. But even this is not standard science, as a wine may be labeled "Cabernet Sauvignon" while also including percentages of other grapes such as Merlot, Malbec, Carmenère, etc. However, in France, the variety of grape rarely appears on the label, where the Château name and place name appear in most imports. Labels from other countries (France, Italy, Spain, etc.) also require a Standard of Quality Indicator such as "Appellation Côtes du Rhône Contrôlée."

1. Brand Identification

Name of Producer / Name of Wine

2. Class, Type or Designation

grape varietal. Designates which grape variety is predominantly used in the wine. In order to qualify as a "Meritage" the wine must be made from a blend of two or more designated grapes, controlled by the Meritage Association. No single variety may make up more than 90% of the total blend. A Red Meritage must include two or more of the following varietals: Cabernet Sauvignon, Merlot, Cabernet Franc, Malbec, Petit Verdot, St. Macaire, Gros Verdot or Carmenère. A White Meritage must include two or more of the following varietals: Sauvignon Blanc, Sémillon or Sauvignon Vert.

appellation of origin. Used to define the location where the grapes were grown for a specific wine. If it is a country, state or county designation, the wine must contain at least 75% of grapes from the Appellation of Origin stated on the label. If an A.V.A. is defined (in the U.S. this is defined, and controlled, by the American Viticultural Area as "delimited grape growing areas"), the wine must contain at least 85% of grapes that were grown in the A.V.A. stated on the label. If a vineyard is designated, at least 95% of the wine must have been made from grapes grown in the designated vineyard (100% if estate is designated).

vintage. Indicates the year of winegrowing, when the grapes were harvested (which many not necessarily be, and often isn't, the same year that the wine was bottled).

3. Who and Where Bottled

The location where the wine was bottled must be listed as "bottled by." Further definitions include:

made and bottled by. The named winery fermented and clarified a minimum of 10% of the wine.

produced and bottled by. The bottler also made at least 75% of the wine by fermenting.

blended and bottled by. The winery mixed the wine with other wine of the same class and type.

cellared, vinted or prepared. These terms indicate that the named winery aged or treated the wine (racking, barrel aging, filtering, etc.) without changing the wine's federal "class" or "type."

4. Country of Origin

Used to designate country of origin. If imported, the importers name and information must also appear.

5. Alcohol Content

Class 1 is designated as Table Wine (any wine having an alcohol content of not less than 7% and not more than 14% by volume). Class 2 is defined as Sparkling Wine. Generally wines under 11% alcohol tend to be sweeter, while those from 11% to 13% tend towards dryness. Wines above 13% or 13.5% alcohol content can go either way.

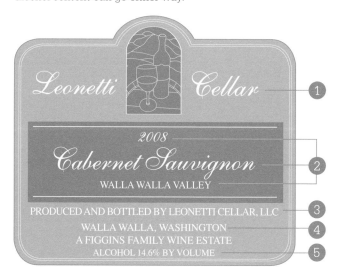

wine bottle sizes

1. 375ml
This designation refers to a small bottle that holds 375ml of wine, half as much as a standard wine container.

2. 750ml
This designation refers to the standard-sized bottle that holds 750ml of wine, or 4/5 quarts. This size bottle, regardless of whether it has a straight or sloping neck, is used for red, white, rosé and sparkling wines. Sparkling wine bottles appear to be larger than standard because they are made of thicker glass to withstand the pressures of carbonation, but they, too, contain 750ml of wine.

3. Magnum
This designation refers to a bottle that holds 1.5 liters of wine, the equivalent of two 750ml bottles. Sparkling wines are sometimes fermented in magnums because this method is believed to lengthen the wine's life.

4. Double Magnum
This designation refers to an oversized bottle that holds three liters of wine, the equivalent of four 750ml bottles.

5. Rehoboam and Jeroboam
The Rehoboam designation refers to an oversized bottle that holds approximately 4.5 liters of wine, the equivalent of six 750ml bottles. The Jeroboam designation refers to an oversized bottle that holds approximately 3 liters of wine, the equivalent of a double magnum or four 750ml bottles. A Jeroboam of still wine is the equivalent of six 750ml bottles or 4.5 liters.

6. Imperial and Methuselah
The Imperial designation refers to an oversized bottle that holds approximately 6 liters of wine, the equivalent of eight 750ml bottles. The Methuselah designation also refers to an oversized bottle that holds the same quantity but is a different shape than the Imperial.

7. Slamanazar
This designation refers to an oversized bottle that holds approximately 9 liters of wine, the equivalent of twelve 750ml bottles.

8. Balthazar
This designation refers to an oversized bottle that holds approximately 12 liters of wine, the equivalent of sixteen 750ml bottles.

9. Nebuchadnezzar
This designation refers to an oversized bottle that holds approximately 13 to 15 liters of wine, depending on the manufacturer, date, country and region of manufacture—this is the equivalent of approximately seventeen to twenty 750ml bottles.

Case
This term refers to a group of 12 750ml or 4/5-quart bottles of wine. A case may consist of a single varietal and vintage year, or it may be a mixed lot of varietals with several vintage dates and/or non-vintage items.

Half Barrel
A half barrel holds 120 750ml bottles of wine, the equivalent of ten cases of twelve 750ml bottles.

Magnum Case
This term refers to a group of six 1.5-liter magnum bottles; each bottle is the equivalent of two 750ml bottles.

Barrel
A full barrel holds 240 750ml bottles of wine, the equivalent of twenty cases of twelve 750ml bottles.

bottle shapes

1. Burgundy Bottle
With more pronounced, sloped shoulders, a Burgundy bottle shape usually denotes Burgundy reds and whites, California Pinot Noirs and most whites, other than Sauvignon Blanc.

2. Bordeaux Bottle
The most frequently used shape, this bottle shape usually denotes Bordeaux reds and whites, Spanish reds, California Cabernets and Merlots.

3. Champagne Bottle
Used for Champagne and sparkling wine, this bottle is made with much thicker glass and a deep punt (the dent at the bottom of the bottle) in order to withstand the pressure of the bubbles or carbonation.

4. Alsace or Hoch Bottle
Most often used for Riesling and Gewurztraminer wines from the regions where the shape originated.

glassware

Great wines deserve great glasses. A wine enthusiast is led by the color, bouquet and taste, but the glass is often sidelined as an instrument to convey the message of the wine. When wine is poured, the bouquet immediately starts to evaporate and its aromas fill the glass in layers according to their density and specific gravity. Every wine has its own blend of fruit, acidity, minerals, tannin and alcohol that are based primarily on the grape variety, climate and soil on which it is grown.

Shape Matters

To fully appreciate the different grape varieties and the characteristics of individual wines, obtain glasses with shapes fine-tuned for the purpose. The shape is responsible for the quality and intensity of the bouquet, as well as the flow of the wine.

Leading glassware designers, like Riedel, make glasses for every type of wine because the glass influences the qualities you taste. For example, a Riesling glass is designed to funnel the wine to the top of the tongue to emphasize its crisp, fruity flavor, then passes the wine over the back of the tongue for a long finish.

Look at the Legs

Swirl the wine around the glass and allow it to settle. The droplets that form and run down the inside of the glass are known as legs, (or as tears in France). Though sometimes taken for a sign of quality, legs instead indicate alcohol content, formed because of the relative evaporation rates of water and alcohol. The slower they move down the glass or the more there are, the higher the alcoholic content. A wine higher in alcohol tends to age better and often feels bigger and richer in the mouth.

Corks, Caps and Closures

Fear not the screw cap! Though cork closures are a long-held, cherished tradition, research has shown that screw caps keep both the seal airtight and the wine fresh, while being easy to remove, replace and produce. Public perception appears to be the only downside for producers. Plastic corks are also gaining in popularity.

choosing the right glass

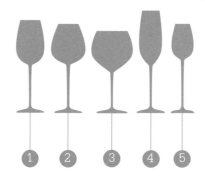

1. Chardonnay
Tapered to enhance freshness and allow mature white wines to express their full range of flavor.

2. Bordeaux
A large bowl intensifies the flavor, aroma and texture, while prolonging the finish.

3. Burgundy
Enhances the fruit, acidity and balance of Burgundy and Pinot Noir. Gives room for the bouquet of the wine to develop in the bowl.

4. Champagne
Emphasizes a stream of bubbles rising, and brings out the bouquet, creaminess and richness of Champagne and sparkling wines.

5. Riesling
Enhances the fruit and balance of this light, acidic wine.

top vintage years by region

KEY: = good   = excellent

REGION	1990	1991	1992	1993	1994	1995	1996	1997	1998	1999	2000	2001	2002	2003	2004	2005	2006	2007	2008	2009
AUSTRALIA red wines	excellent	excellent			good		good		excellent	good	good	good	excellent		excellent	good	good	good		
FRANCE alsace	excellent				good	good			good		good	excellent			excellent	excellent		excellent	good	
FRANCE red bordeaux: médoc	excellent					good	good				excellent	good		good	good	excellent			good	good
FRANCE red bordeaux: graves/pessac-léognan	excellent				good	good			good		excellent	good			good	excellent			good	excellent
FRANCE red bordeaux: pomerol	excellent				good	good			excellent		excellent	good			good	excellent			good	excellent
FRANCE red bordeaux: saint-émilion	excellent					good			excellent		excellent	good			good	excellent			good	excellent
FRANCE white bordeaux: sauternes and barsac	excellent							good		good	excellent	excellent				excellent				
FRANCE red burgandy: côte de beaune	excellent						good			excellent			good	good		excellent				excellent
FRANCE red burgandy: côte de nuits	excellent						good			excellent			excellent	good		excellent				excellent
FRANCE white burgundy	excellent		good			excellent	good				excellent		excellent		good	good				excellent
FRANCE champagne	excellent					excellent	good			excellent			excellent						excellent	
FRANCE central loire (vouvray, côteaux du layon, quart de chaumes, savennières, etc.)							good	good			good	excellent	good	excellent	good	good		good		
FRANCE eastern loire (sancerre, pouilly-fumé, etc.)	good					good	excellent	good					good		excellent	good		good	good	
FRANCE northern rhône (hermitage, côte rôtie, corras, etc.)	good	good			good	good			good	excellent		good		excellent	excellent	excellent	good			
FRANCE southern rhône (châteauneuf-du-pape, gigondas, côtes du rhône, etc.)	excellent					good			excellent	good	excellent	excellent		excellent	excellent	excellent	excellent	excellent		excellent
GERMANY	excellent		good	good	good				good	good		good	good	good	good	good		good		
ITALY piedmont	excellent					excellent	excellent	excellent	good	excellent	good	excellent		good	excellent		excellent	good		
ITALY tuscany	good				good	excellent		excellent		good					excellent		excellent	excellent		
PORTUGAL vintage port		good	good		excellent			good			excellent			excellent				excellent		
SPAIN rioja					good	excellent	good					excellent			excellent	good	good			
SPAIN rivera del duero						good	excellent		good			excellent			excellent	good	excellent	good		
UNITED STATES california cabernet sauvignon	excellent	good	good		excellent	good						excellent	excellent	good		good		good		
UNITED STATES california chardonnay						good		good					excellent	excellent		excellent	good			
UNITED STATES california pinot noir									good		good		excellent	excellent	excellent		excellent	good		
UNITED STATES california syrah											good		excellent	excellent	excellent		good			
UNITED STATES california zinfandel	good	good	excellent	good	good							excellent	good			good		good		
UNITED STATES oregon pinot noir	good		good	good	excellent				good	excellent			excellent		good		excellent		good	
UNITED STATES washington cabernet sauvignon and merlot									good	excellent	good	excellent	good			excellent	excellent			

resources

chef biographies

Culled from our own breathtaking backyard along the Big Wood River and from some of the finest and most famous kitchens in the world, *Entertaining Sun Valley Style: Behind the Scenes from the Sun Valley Center Wine Auction*—just like the world-famous wine auction it honors—is a celebration of culinary excellence. The recipes that comprise this book were created by some of the country's top chefs. They are men and women who have a passion for pairing great wine with great food.

Sky Barker
Executive Chef, Zōu 75

Born and raised in the Wood River Valley, Sky Barker's earliest food memory was at age 11 when he ordered chicken noodle soup at the Western Culinary Institute in Portland, Oregon. "It was a simple dish," Sky recalls vividly, "but the noodles were different, the flavor blending perfect and the presentation unique."

That dish began a lifelong passion for food that has translated into training and guidance with some of the most venerable chefs in the Wood River Valley. Barker also apprenticed under head chef Earnest Oullet at Zōu 75, whom he credits with teaching him the basic tenets of advanced technique and instilling a sense of discipline in the kitchen.

After nearly a decade at Zōu 75, executive chef Sky Barker continues to be inspired to create unique and flavorful dishes by using simple, fresh and honest ingredients. Cilantro and jalapeno peppers are two of his favorite spices, although he is best known for his subtle and tantalizing scallop creations that combine French infusion cooking with traditional Japanese techniques and ingredients. The result is a creative combination of flavors that has helped Zōu 75 forge a name locally and nationally for inventive specialty dishes.

"Food is an artistic expression of atmosphere, service, presentation and taste," Chef Barker asserts, "and music, art and food go together as an experience."

Cristina Ceccatelli Cook
Proprietor, Cristina's Restaurant

"I am a proud *Toscanaccia*, a Tuscan troublemaker, as the other Italians call us. We Tuscans invented the fork and followed it up with Dante, Michelangelo, and the Renaissance," says Cristina Ceccatelli Cook, the owner and self-professed "cook" of Cristina's Restaurant in Ketchum. "We believe in Destiny, pasta, wine, our mothers, friends, love . . . and, of course, soccer."

For 18 years, Cristina's Restaurant has been cooking and baking for enthusiastic customers who come to the charming, salmon-colored house in Ketchum to enjoy the company of friends, good conversation, and fresh, satisfying food.

Cristina's philosophy is simple: to re-create the Italian sense of fun and camaraderie, celebrating life with a good meal in good company. "In Tuscany our lives are centered around the table. Italians say that spending time at the table brings longevity, perhaps because all the senses come alive with colors, aromas and tastes, not to mention the joking and laughing. It's not just about food . . . it's about fellowship."

Cristina is the author of two successful cookbooks, *Cristina's of Sun Valley* and *Cristina's Tuscan Table*, which was selected as one of *Food & Wine* magazine's favorite 25 cookbooks of the year for 2007 and featured in their annual Best of the Best cookbook.

Derek Holliday
Sushi Chef, Zōu 75

A descendant of Wild West gunslinger, Doc Holliday, Derek Holliday is a six-foot four-inch, knife-wielding head sushi chef with eyes greener than the Irish blood flowing through his veins.

Hailing from Coeur d'Alene, Idaho, Derek is well-traveled and has spent many years fishing the Pacific Ocean, from the coast of Los Angeles to the Arctic Circle. Eventually wandering back to the Wood River, Derek found his way to Zōu 75 where he apprenticed under Japanese Master Chef Motohiko Sato for four years. Using his great knowledge, experience, and commitment to tradition, Derek went on to command the helm that is the sushi line at Zōu 75.

Applying French infusion cooking to traditional Japanese recipes and techniques, Zōu 75 has forged a name for itself not only locally, but on the national scene as one of the most creative, consistent, and celebrated restaurants around. With fresh fish flown in several times a week straight from Honolulu, Hawaii, the master chefs at Zōu 75 work with the best in quality and freshness, allowing them to craft a wide variety of unique and inventive rolls and specialty dishes with that unique Zōu 75 signature and flair.

Chris Kastner
Proprietor and Chef, CK's Real Food

CK are the initials of Chris Kastner, chef and partner with Rebecca, his wife of twenty-four years. Together, they have been in the restaurant business for thirty-four years. Chris started as a dish washer at the Sun Valley Inn in 1976 and has been working in kitchens ever since. After working mostly in the Ketchum area at the late and widely acclaimed Evergreen and Chez Russell, Chris and Rebecca decided to do their own thing and opened CK's Real Food in Hailey in 2003, as an independently owned and operated dinner house, open seven nights a week all year. CK's recently opened for lunch Monday through Friday, with a focus on serving affordable, quality lunches.

"Regional Northwest cuisine is what we do. We emphasize the use of as much local organic produce in season as possible and, by using local and regional foods and drawing inspiration from different cuisines around the world, we create tasty and healthy dishes to complement our extensive wine list. Our menu changes a little bit all the time depending on the season, although some items do not change due to their popularity."

Rebecca has developed the dessert menu and runs most of the business, as well as being on the floor most nights. Chris is in the kitchen most nights and oversees all menu development with the help of his great staff. CK's is a family affair with Gavin and Simone, their grown-up children, having a hand in the operation too. Simone makes all the ice creams and sorbets, and works the line. Gavin works in the kitchen and the dining room. The Kastners have a strong local following of customers who enjoy and appreciate the tasty and healthy cuisine CK's brings to their tables every time they come to dine.

CONSTANTINOS LALIOTITIS: WWW.ALANCAMPBELLPHOTOGRAPHY.COM

Constantinos "Taki" Laliotitis
Executive Chef, Jackson Family Wines

Chef Constantinos "Taki" Laliotitis had some excellent training before he became the chef for Jackson Family Wines. As a kid he was the official taste tester of his mom's traditional Greek dishes. Taki's parents were in the restaurant business, and he vividly remembers the food, wine and festive atmosphere of the family's weekly dinner parties. "I've always known food and wine to be a cause for celebration," says Taki. "It's about bringing people together and sharing the experience with family and friends."

While Chef Taki's culinary journey started in the family kitchen, his appreciation for wine began as a student at the prestigious École Supérieure de Cuisine Française in Paris. During his studies he traveled the globe to learn about the connection between a wine's growing region and the cuisine served there. "When you understand the wine and the region that it comes from," says Taki, "you can see why people in different parts of the world eat a certain way, and why certain pairings are timeless and classic."

Chef Taki has created extraordinary meals at world-class restaurants in France, Italy, Japan, and throughout California— including the legendary French Laundry in Napa. This global résumé gives him a broad knowledge of international cuisine, and allows him to "bring the proper experiences to the situation at hand."

As the chef for Jackson Family Wines, he strives to "frame food around the wine," to enhance the experience and enjoyment of both elements. "I want to prepare dishes simply, let the ingredients have a voice, and make the relationship between food and wine special." Just don't ask Taki to cook Greek food. "I don't do it too much," Taki says with a chuckle. "I still can't top my mom's old recipes."

Sarah Lipton
Pastry Chef, SEGO Restaurant & Bar

Pastry Chef Sarah Lipton is inventive. She is known for producing desserts that are not only delicious, but also charming. Her recent creations have included bacon doughnuts, homemade marshmallows, ice cream cookie sandwiches, chocolate pretzel tarts and Bailey's ice cream. And that is only a sampling of the evolving dessert menu she has created in her time as pastry chef and kitchen manager at Ketchum's SEGO Restaurant and Bar.

Lipton returned to her childhood vacation home in 2009 to work at SEGO crafting desserts and unique confections for the highly inventive menu. Prior to that she worked as the pastry assistant at the St. Regis Hotel in Aspen and as pastry chef at Aspen's acclaimed institution, The Little Nell. Trained at the French Pastry School in Chicago, with a Bachelor's Degree in Hospitality Business at Michigan State University, Sarah has worked in kitchens across the country, from Boston to Chicago, Aspen, Colorado, Laguna Beach, California and most recently, Ketchum, Idaho. She now calls Ketchum home, enjoying the slopes, lakes, mountains and community of the Wood River Valley. As SEGO's pastry chef she has been challenged, educated, and is a proud member of a kitchen team that produces local, seasonal, biodynamic, handmade food. Her magical and delicious creations follow that philosophy and expand upon it as a way to complete your dining experience.

Beau MacMillan
Executive Chef, elements restaurant, Sanctuary on Camelback Mountain

As executive chef of Sanctuary on Camelback Mountain in Arizona and its signature restaurant, elements, Beau MacMillan inspires his staff with his passion for fresh ingredients. His ingenuity in the kitchen is stimulated by his belief that food should not be overworked, but rather appreciated for its simplicity and natural perfection. This philosophy is evident in Chef MacMillan's innovative seasonal menus that focus on fresh, local ingredients procured from a network of artisans and organic farmers.

Chef MacMillan, who hails from Plymouth, Massachusetts, has cooked in some of America's most distinguished kitchens. His culinary career began at the age of 16 when he secured a position at Crane Brook Tea Room in Carver, Massachusetts. Chef MacMillan spent a year under the tutelage of Chef Francois de Melogue. Inspired by this experience, he joined the brigade at La Vieille Maison in Boca Raton, Florida, before being drawn to the culinary scene on the West Coast, where he held sous chef positions at the prestigious Hotel Bel Air, and later Shutters on the Beach in Santa Monica. He was then recruited to Arizona to develop the cuisine at The Ranch on Camelback, which later became Sanctuary on Camelback Mountain. Chef MacMillan and Chef Charles Wiley opened elements in March of 2001.

As executive chef, MacMillan's innovation has brought elements national recognition and acclaim. In March 2006, Chef MacMillan was invited to The Food Network's kitchen stadium to compete in an episode of the hit series, "Iron Chef America." Pitted against Iron Chef Bobby Flay in "Battle American Kobe Beef," Chef MacMillan's cuisine ultimately reigned supreme, letting him claim victory over Flay.

Chef MacMillan is the co-host of The Food Network's hit series "Worst Cooks in America" along with "Secrets of a Restaurant Chef: Anne Burrell" which premiered in January 2010. Beau has also appeared on NBC's "Today Show" numerous times and has cooked at The James Beard House and at *Bon Appétit* magazine in New York.

Scott Mason
Proprietor and Chef, Ketchum Grill

Scott started out where all great restaurateurs begin, at the bottom—bussing tables and washing dishes. But also like them, he didn't stay there for long. Over his thirty-five-year career Scott has done it all: cooking alongside master chefs, apprenticing in the kitchens of France, leading daily menu creation, and so much more. In addition to being the creative force behind Ketchum Grill, he is the author of numerous articles related to food and cooking, an expert in local wild mushrooms and an accomplished wine steward. He even provides Valley residents with the "food tip of the week" on local radio station, KECH.

A native of Eugene, Oregon, Scott worked alongside German Master Chef Norbert Schultz at Santa Barbara's prestigious Norbert's and at the well-known San Ysidro Ranch, where he met his wife Anne, a pastry chef. Together they partnered with Norbert to open two other restaurants in three years, Brigittes, and then Oysters, before moving to Marin County where Scott became the head Chef of Alessia Restaurant under the tutelage of Guido Piccinini, a thirty-year veteran of Italian kitchens. In 1989 Scott and his growing family moved to Sun Valley where Scott became the Chef at Freddy's Taverne D'Alsace and also the lead chef at well-regarded Soupçon. In 1991, Scott purchased Taverne D' Alsace at the historic Ed Williams House and—with Freddy's blessing—re-opened as the Ketchum Grill. Scott continues to guide the Ketchum Grill with this dedication and hard work and with an abundant gratitude for our extraordinary local community and environment.

Judith McQueen
Proprietor and Chef, Judith McQueen Entertaining

It's no understatement to call Judith McQueen a legendary Sun Valley chef . . . ask around, it's true. Her relentless pursuit of marrying food and beauty is both her calling card and her passion. Judith's current endeavor, the catering and entertainment company she founded in 1998, Judith McQueen Entertaining, is the culmination of thirty-three years of hands-on food service experience, including twenty-three years as a professionally chef and six years in corporate food service, as well as nearly two decades of event and party planning and corporate functions.

Judith McQueen Entertaining sets the standard for exquisite catering and event planning both in Sun Valley, Idaho, and beyond. "We pride ourselves on exquisite presentations and luscious flavors," says Judith.

Judith has wined and dined heads of state, celebrities, captains of industry, and more often than not, dear, dear friends. Comfortable dealing with a myriad of cultural and regional cuisines, Judith likens her client's initial experience to a kid in a candy shop—if you can dream it, it can be done.

The perfection is in the details and Judith McQueen Entertaining delivers unparalleled service, tailor-made cuisine and pitch-perfect atmosphere every time, so that your affair—whether a wedding, a shower or an intimate dinner with your closest friends—is a memorable one.

Taite Pearson
Executive Chef, SEGO Restaurant & Bar

Taite Pearson's culinary path has been forged through determination and cultural curiosity, combined with a natural affinity for cooking and a learning-by-doing work ethic. Food was always part of the family dynamic when he was growing up in Colorado, and he cooked frequently as a child.

Pearson's ambition to become a chef inspired him to set out to cook in some of the best kitchens in Arizona, and he landed his first sous chef position at the age of 20 at Wright's at the Arizona Biltmore. Positions at a number of esteemed restaurants in Phoenix and Tucson—including Mary Elaine's, the Ventana Room, and Janos—followed.

Moving to Chicago in 1997, Pearson worked as a sous chef at the venerable Charlie Trotter's before moving to Brasserie T, where he was executive sous chef. He returned to Tucson in 2000 and opened his own restaurant, Linen. There, he refined his technique, creating degustation-focused, modern French cuisine. Linen received great acclaim and Pearson was credited with setting the standard for restaurants in the Southwest.

The need to flex his culinary muscles in a bigger, more diverse city led Pearson to Las Vegas in 2002, where he once again proved his mettle, working as chef de cuisine for Wolfgang Puck's Postrio, Spago, and Wolfgang Puck Bar and Grill. He moved to Joël Robuchon at The Mansion in 2005, helping the renowned establishment earn its Michelin three-star rating before returning to the Wolfgang Puck Fine Dining Group as executive chef and director of culinary development.

"Being a chef is often about adaptation and understanding the environment in which you are practicing your craft," Pearson says. To that end, when he moved to southern California in 2007, he took on a series of new challenges, including working as the private chef to Mr. David Geffen, before accepting the challenge of executive chef in opening SEGO Restaurant and Bar in Ketchum in 2009.

Duane Runswick
Executive Chef, Feast Catering

Born in San Francisco into a family of foodies, Duane Runswick's love of cooking started at an early age. His fate was sealed when he landed his first kitchen job washing dishes at age 13 and was promoted to line cook shortly afterward.

After cooking his way through college in northern California, Runswick eventually attended culinary school in Portland, Oregon. It was a significant location, as this is where he was first exposed to the then fledgling farm to table movement, which forever altered his general approach to food and method of cooking each dish.

Craving more experience and hands-on education with master chefs after culinary school, Runswick joined the opening staff at the St Regis Monarch Beach in southern California where he came into his own under the guidance of some incredible chef mentors.

"I prefer cooking from the hip, rather than planning out menus weeks in advance," says Chef Runswick, "because it allows me to use fresh, local ingredients as opposed to far-flung provisions from around the world." Chef Runswick's favorite style of cuisine is French-inspired California cuisine, but his strong background and interest in Italian cuisine leads to a melding of flavors and dishes that is fresh, yet traditional, using honest ingredients that are sourced locally whenever possible.

"I love Idaho," adds Chef Runswick. "It's a fantastic place to cook, because of all of the fresh local ingredients."

Ben Spungin
Pastry Chef, Marinus at Bernardus Lodge

For the past five years, Ben Spungin has been working alongside Chef Cal Stamenov to develop pastry creations that compliment Stamenov's signature California natural cuisine at Bernardus Lodge in Carmel Valley, California.

Originally from Durham, North Carolina, Ben started his culinary career at 16, working at the acclaimed Foster's Market. This experience of 'simple harvest food' gave Ben a foundation to base his ideals and ambitions. In 1996, Ben attended the New England Culinary Institute in Montpelier, Vermont, earning his Associates degree. Ben's school internship was at the Magnolia Grill in Durham under James Beard Award-winning Chefs Ben and Karen Barker. After finishing school in 1998, a spontaneous opportunity opened at the French Laundry to work under pastry chef Stephen Durfee and pastry sous Shuna Lydon. This adventure opened Ben's eyes to the endless possibilities of the pastry world.

Two years later, inspired by the coast and the microclimates around the Monterey Peninsula, Ben took the pastry chef position at the Post Ranch Inn in Big Sur, quickly developing an interest in wild and foraged ingredients.

In 2005, Ben became the pastry chef at the Bernardus Lodge under Chef Cal Stamenov. Chef Cal, a former pastry chef himself, and Ben have a collaborative relationship anchored by their passion for quality ingredients. Chef Cal's relationship with local foragers and farmers keeps an ever-changing menu alive in the kitchen and provides Ben with the ability to create without any limitations.

Ben currently lives on the Big Sur coastline with his wife and two adorable little girls.

Cal Stamenov
Culinary Director and Chef, Marinus at Bernardus Lodge

Upon graduating from the California Culinary Academy, Cal Stamenov began his career in 1982 at New York's famed Four Seasons restaurant. He is steeped in the European tradition of culinary artistry and has spent years in the most demanding kitchens of the world's most renowned chefs. His stellar credits include working with Alain Ducasse of the three-star Michelin restaurant, Louis XV at the Hotel de Paris, Monaco; Pierre Gagnaire in St. Étienne, France; Masa Koboiashi at Masa's Restaurant in San Francisco; Jean-Louis Palladin at Restaurant Jean-Louis in Washington D.C.; and Michel Richard at Citrus Restaurant. Stamenov worked as executive chef for the Highlands Inn in Carmel, and served as chef de cuisine of the highly regarded Domaine Chandon Restaurant in Napa Valley.

Marinus at Bernardus Lodge, which resembles an Old World wine country estate and is graced by a dramatic 12-foot wide European fireplace with a raised hearth, offering spectacular views of the garden, majestic pines and nearby California oaks, has been enjoying high praise since the resort opened in 1999. The Zagat Survey has noted Marinus as one of the Top Restaurants and Most Romantic places south of San Francisco and it has won Wine Spectator magazine's highly coveted "Grand Award" for its wine cellar since 2001. Since 1981, only 89 restaurants from 12 countries have earned the Grand Award, an honor bestowed every three years.

Cal's philosophy and style of cooking is built on three central pillars: the relationship between food and terroir, the superiority of handcrafted, artisanal products chosen over mass-produced, and the common sense of glorifying food when its flavor is at its peak. He also has his own organic herb and vegetable gardens and vineyards at Bernardus Lodge. With a treasure trove of impeccable products, Stamenov is able to cook with the seasons and rarely has to look further than his own backyard for inspiration.

John Tesar
Culinary Director, The Cedars Social; Chef, Dallas Restaurant Group (DRG) Concepts

Widely known for his sustainable food ethics and mastery of seafood, John Tesar most recently has returned to Texas to consult for DRG Concepts in Dallas. He is currently opening a cocktail den and comfort food kitchen called The Cedars Social in downtown Dallas with former NFL star Brian Williams. Chef Tesar, also known as "Jimmy Sears" in Anthony Bourdain's books "Kitchen Confidential" and "Medium Raw," has worked and owned restaurants in New York City and northern California and was executive chef at Rick Moonen RM Seafood in New York and Las Vegas.

Chef Tesar is currently charged with the creation of new restaurant menus for DRG, along with the continued menu development of three existing restaurant brands including: Dallas Chop House, Dallas Fish Market and Fish Express. John's recent acclaim for "Best Burger in Houston" for his former namesake restaurant, Tesar's, has catapulted his interest in the national development of Chop House Burger Bar for DRG Concepts. John will soon release his cookbook, *The Modern Texas Beef Cookbook Crafted by Chef John Tesar*.

Bringing his "stylish, contemporary American cuisine prepared with European techniques," the five-star chef's critical acclaim came to the forefront during his work as executive chef for the Rosewood Mansion on Turtle Creek. Under Chef Tesar's leadership, John Mariani named the Mansion Restaurant one of the top new restaurants in America in *Esquire's* November 2008 issue. Tesar also achieved five stars for the Mansion Restaurant from the *Dallas Morning News* food critic, Bill Addison and freelance food critic Dotty Griffith. And Nancy Nichols of *D Magazine* named the restaurant one of the Top Ten of 2008. He has appeared on "The Early Show," "The Today Show," and cooked at the James Beard House in September 2010 for the seventh time.

Along with the chef's numerous awards and accolades, John Tesar was a semi-finalist for the 2009 James Beard Award for "Best Chef: Southwest" and is one of five chefs in the country to serve on Share our Strength's Taste of the Nation National Culinary Council.

Susan Zemanick
Executive Chef, Gautreau's Restaurant

Susan Zemanick began her culinary career at the early age of fifteen while working in fine dining restaurants in Wilkes-Barre, Pennsylvania. She quickly realized that cooking was her passion and calling. After high school she enrolled at The Culinary Institute of America in Hyde Park, New York. Upon graduating in the top of her class, she was offered a position to work one-on-one with a Chef-Instructor as a fellow in the seafood department. During that fellowship she developed a great love for fish and seafood, which brought her to New Orleans.

Upon arriving in New Orleans she began cooking at Commander's Palace. She later moved on to work at Gautreau's Restaurant, under Top Ten Food and Wine winner, Mat Wolf. After working her way up the ranks she was promoted to executive chef in 2005. In 2007 the *Times-Picayune* named her one of "Seven Chefs to Watch." Since that time, she was named "Chef of the Year" by *New Orleans Magazine* in 2008, has been an Award Finalist for James Beard's "Rising Star Chef" in both 2009 and 2010 and was named a "2008 Top Ten Best New Chef in America" by *Food & Wine* magazine.

Gautreau's offers modern French and contemporary Louisiana fare using only the freshest ingredients.

vintner menus

The following are the actual and complete menus presented at the Vintner Dinners by the chefs and vineyards.

Blanding Residence 2009

Reception
Foie Blond with Toasted Brioche, Apricot Confit
Blue Fin Tuna Tartare with Black Truffle Vinaigrette
Rice Paper Vegetable Roll with Yuzu Citrus Sauce
Warm Parmesan Gougères

2006 Schramsberg Brut Rosé

1st Course
California Vegetable Salad
with Heirloom Tomato, Pole Beans, Goat Cheese Croutons,
Sauce Ravigote

2007 DeLille Cellars Chaleur Estate Blanc

2nd Course
Monterey Bay Red Abalone
with White Summer Corn, Winter Black Truffle Sauce

2007 Chappellet Napa Valley Chardonnay

3rd Course
Porcini and Chanterelle
with Thyme Roasted, Parsley Root Agnolotti, Bacon Shallot
Beurre Rouge

2005 Chappellet Syrah
2005 DeLille Cellars Doyenne Syrah

4th Course
Alder Smoked Sonoma Duck
with Almond Risotto, Roasted Mission Fig, Balsamic Duck Jus
2006 Chappellet Merlot
2005 DeLille Cellars Doyenne AIX

5th Course
Wagyu Beef Rib-Eye
Pomme Ancienne, Roasted Torpedo Onion, Béarnaise

*2006 Chappellet Pritchard Hill Estate Vineyard
Cabernet Sauvignon*
2005 DeLille Cellars Grand Ciel Cabernet Sauvignon

6th Course / Dessert
Summer Fruits
with Roasted Apricot, Strawberries, Honeysuckle Ice Cream
Petit Fours

1998 Chappellet Chenin Blanc Liqueroux

232 entertaining sun valley style

Booth Residence 2010

Reception
2008 Freemark Abbey Viognier

1st Course
Butter Poached Maine Lobster,
Lightly Smoked Yukon Gold Potato Ravioli,
Arrowhead Spinach, Frothy Mustard Infused Nage

2008 Hartford Court Stone Côte Chardonnay

2nd Course
Thyme Infused Liberty Farms Duck,
Tokyo Turnips, Foie Gras, Roasted Sweet Plums,
Toasted Sesame

2006 La Jota Howell Mountain Merlot

3rd Course
Grilled Kobe Tri-tip Trifolata, Shallot Confiture,
Sweet Corn, Porcini Mushroom Heritage Barley Casserole,
Sauce Perigourdine

2006 Cardinale

4th Course / Dessert
Gianduja Chocolate Mousse, Feuilletine,
Blackberry Pâte de Fruit, Hazelnut Crème Anglaise

2006 Hartford Court Late Harvest Zinfandel

Brown Residence 2010

1st Course
Goat Cheese Blinis
Foie Gras Torchon

Domaine Serene "R" Rosé

2nd Course
Jumbo Lump Crab, Gnocchi, Chanterelle Mushrooms,
English Peas and Parmesan Cream

2007 Domaine Serene Côte Sud Vineyard Chardonnay

3rd Course
Sautéed Arctic Char, Roasted Fingerling Potatoes,
Haricots Verts and Dijon Crème Fraîche

2006 Domaine Serene Evenstad Reserve Pinot Noir

4th Course
Roasted Quail Stuffed with Foie Gras and Poached Pears,
Sautéed Swiss Chard and Sangiovese Reduction

2007 Leonetti Cellar Sangiovese

5th Course
Pistachio Crusted Rack of Lamb,
Bloomsdale Spinach, Cherry Lamb Demi-Glace

2007 Leonetti Cellar Cabernet

6th Course / Dessert
Crème Sophia, Fresh Raspberries, Lemon Verbena Sauce

Heinz Residence 2010

1st Course
Black Cod with Basil and Rose Petal Pesto
Summer Squash and Sweet Onions
(Merluzzo con Pesto di Basilico e Petali di Rose)

2009 Poet's Leap Riesling

2nd Course
Asparagus Folded Lasagna
(Lasagna di Asparagi)

2007 Folonari Saggi

3rd Course
Granita allo Champagne

4th Course
Pork Osso Buco with Porchetta Rub
(Osso Buco di Maiale con Spezie alla Porchetta)

2007 Meteor Cabernet

5th Course
Figs, le Chevrot and Nut Crostino
(Fichi, le Chevrot e Crostino di Noci)

2006 Pedestal Merlot

6th Course / Dessert
Chocolate Tartufo
(Tartufo al Cioccolato)

2006 Sequel Syrah

Mott Residence 2010

Reception
Seasonal selection of assorted canapes

2009 Lachini Vineyards Rosé, Willamette Valley Amuse Bouche
2009 Lachini Vineyards Pinot Gris

1st Course
Tuna Tartare
Osetra Caviar, Yuzu, Green Onion Potato Pancakes

2008 Lachini Vineyards Family Estate Pinot Noir
2008 Pinot Noir, Cuvée Giselle

2nd Course
Smoked Kurobuta Pork Belly
Tempura Crisps, Local Vegetable Salad, Poached Organic Egg

Lachini Vineyards Library Pinot Noir

3rd Course
Wild Mushroom Risotto
Aged Reggiano, Black Truffle
2007 Facets of Gemstone Estate Red Blend

4th Course
Snake River Farms American Kobe Beef Filet
Leek and Goat Cheese Tater Tot, Foie Gras

2006 Gemstone Estate Cabernet Sauvignon

5th Course / Dessert
Chilled Passion Fruit Soup
with Avocado, Coconut and Basil

Nelson Residence 2008

1st Course
Sustainable Bigeye Tuna Foie Gras Tourchon with
Sea Salt and Riviera Ligure Olive Oil

2007 Villa Creek, Proprietary White

2nd Course
Maine Lobster Ravioli, Uni Butter
and Salmon Trout Roe

2006 Chappellet Chardonnay

3rd Course
Pulled Short Rib, Potato Gnocchi, Baby Peas
and Wild Mushrooms

2005 Chappellet Pritchard Hill Cabernet Sauvignon

4th Course
Herb and Garlic-Crusted Rack of Veal, Roasted Baby
Vegetable and Creamed Potato Salad

2006 Villa Creek, Willow Creek Cuvée

5th Course
Selection of Dry-Aged Cheeses

2005 Villa Creek, Onda

6th Course / Dessert
Poached Texas Peaches, Honey Mousse,
Sable Breton and White Peach Sorbet
Assorted Chocolates

1998 Chappellet Liqueroux

Vogel Residence 2010

1st Course
Foie Gras
Figs and Duck Prosciutto
Melon

2006 Trefethen Dry Reisling

2nd Course
Idaho Caviar with Corn Pudding, Brioche, Quail Egg

2007 Trefethen Chardonnay

3rd Course
Golden Trout with Fennel, Mustard, Tomato

2008 Booker "White" Roussane, Viognier

4th Course
Confit Rabbit with Sausage, Hand Rolled Pasta, Black Raspberries

2008 Booker "Fracture" Syrah

5th Course
Pork Cheek and Belly
with Chanterelles, Romanesco, Bordelaise

2005 Trefethen Cabernet Sauvignon

6th Course / Dessert
Olive Oil Cake, Red Wine Plums, Pluot Sorbet

2008 Booker "The Ripper" Grenache

sources

Local Markets
Many of these products are available through, or can be ordered by, our local markets.

Atkinsons' Markets
(Bellevue, Hailey and Ketchum)
208.726.5668
www.atkinsons.com

CIRO Market & Wine Merchants
Ketchum, ID
208.622.4400
www.cirosunvalley.com

Idaho's Bounty
208.721.8074
www.idahosbounty.org

Hailey Farmer's Market
Thursdays, 2:30 to 6:30 pm
June through October

Ketchum Farmer's Market
Tuesdays, 2:30 to 6 pm
June through October

Wood River Farmer's Markets
www.wrfarmersmarket.org

Cheese and Dairy
Atkinsons' Markets
(Bellevue, Hailey and Ketchum)
208.726.5668
www.atkinsons.com

CIRO Market & Wine Merchants
Ketchum, ID
208.622.4400
www.cirosunvalley.com

Rogue Creamery Blue Cheese
The Rogue Creamery
Central Point, OR
866.396.4704
www.roguecreamery.com

Toscano Fresco
Cristina's Restaurant
Ketchum, ID
208.726.4499

Condiments, Vinegars, Syrups
Agreste
Cristina's Restaurant
Ketchum, ID
208.726.4499

Japanese Mayonnaise
Amazon.com
www.amazon.com

Mirin (sweet rice wine)
Atkinsons' Markets
(Bellevue, Hailey and Ketchum)

Pomegranate Molasses
igourmet.com
www.igourmet.com

Saba Wine Syrup
Cristina's Restaurant
Ketchum, ID
208.726.4499

Gourmet-Food.com
770.485.0878
www.gourmet-food.com

Desserts and Pastry
Gianduja Chocolate
igourmet.com
www.igourmet.com

Pastry Cream Powder
Rader Foods
800.223.1103
www.raderfoods.com

TCHO Chocolate
San Francisco, CA
415.981.0189
www.tcho.com

Fish and Shellfish
Abalone
Catalina Offshore Products
San Diego, CA
619.704.3639
www.catalinaop.com

Arctic Char
I Love Blue Sea
415.300.0940
www.ilovebluesea.com

Caviar
Atkinsons' Markets
(Bellevue, Hailey and Ketchum)
www.atkinsons.com

Gourmet Food Store
www.gourmetfoodstore.com

Caviar Line
www.caviar-line.com

Sun Valley Smoked Trout
Atkinsons' Market
(Bellevue, Hailey and Ketchum)
208.726.5668
www.atkinsons.com

Sun Valley Smoked Trout
www.smokedtrout.com

Fruits and Vegetables
Bing Cherries
Cherrystone Orchard
Emmett, ID
208.365.2344
www.applesandcherries.com

Black Truffle
Atkinsons' Market
(Ketchum location)
www.atkinsons.com

Caviar Line
www.caviar-line.com

Gourmet Food Store
www.gourmetfoodstore.com

Marx Foods Wholesale Online
www.marxfoods.com

Huckleberries
Northwest Wild Foods
Burlington, WA
360.757.7940
www.nwwildfoods.com

Wild Mountain Berries
Riggins, ID
208.628.3594
www.wildmountainberries.com

Romanesco
Marx Foods Wholesale Online
866.588.6279
www.marxfoods.com

Wood River Farmer's Markets
www.wrfarmersmarket.org

Tuscan Kale
Wood River Farmer's Markets
www.wrfarmersmarket.org

Verjus Juice
Fusion Verjus
www.verjus.com

Terra Sonoma Food Company
707.431.1382
www.terrasonoma.com

Wild Mushrooms/
Mushroom Dust
(Chanterelles, Morel, Porcini Truffles)

Atkinsons' Markets
(Bellevue, Hailey and Ketchum)
208.726.5668
www.atkinsons.com

D'Artagnan
800.327.8246
www.dartagnan.com

Marx Foods Wholesale Online
866.588.6279
www.marxfoods.com

Wood River Farmer's Markets
www.wrfarmersmarket.org

Yuzu Sauce
Marx Foods Wholesale Online
www.marxfoods.com

Simply Natural
www.simply-natural.biz

Yuzu Fruit
Amazon.com
www.amazon.com

Exotic Fruit Market
www.exoticfruitmarket.com
951.657.7299

Gourmet Sleuth
www.gourmetsleuth.com

Meats and Game
Duck Prosciutto
Italia Gourmet
510.205.2651
www.italia-gourmet.com

Wally's Wine and Spirits
Los Angeles, CA
888.9.WALLYS
www.wallywine.com

Elk Tenderloin
Black Canyon Elk Ranch
Emmett, ID
208.365.5432
www.blackcanyonelk.com

CA Bull Elk Ranch
Hazelton, ID
208.404.9632
www.cabullelkranch.com

Cowboy Free Range Meat
Jackson Hole, WY
866.435.5411
www.cowboyfreerangemeat.com

Kobe Beerf
Snake River Farms
Boise, ID
877.736.0193
www.snakeriverfarms.com

Kurobuta Pork
Snake River Farms
Boise, ID
877.736.0193
www.snakeriverfarms.com

Lamb
Lava Lake Lamb
Hailey, ID
www.lavalakelamb.com
208.788.1710, 888.528.5253

Rabbit
Idaho's Bounty
208.721.8074
www.idahosbounty.org

Mountain View Rabbitry
Cascade, ID
208.382.4659
www.ozmer.com

Rabbit Legs (Braised)
D'Artagnan
800.327.8246
www.dartagnan.com

Specialty
Honeysuckle Flowers
Ketchum Kitchens
Ketchum, ID
208.726.1989, 800.992.4860
www.ketchumkitchens.com

Marx Foods Wholesale Online
866.588.6279
www.marxfoods.com

Catering
Feast Catering
Duane Runswick
Ketchum, ID
208.726.0626

Judith McQueen Entertaining
Hailey, ID
208.788.7716
www.judithmcqueen.com

Rasberrys Catering
Ketchum, ID
208.726.0606
Hailey, ID
208.928.7711
www.rasberrysonline.com

Tabletop, Florists and Entertaining
Barbara's Party Rentals
Ketchum, ID
208.726.3778
www.barbaraspartyrental.com

Botanica
Kurt McCauley
208.720.1170
kurmen@aol.com

Ketchum Flower Company
Ketchum, ID
208.622.7364
www.ketchumflowers.com

Ketchum Kitchens
Ketchum, ID
208.726.1989, 800.992.4860
www.ketchumkitchens.com

Primavera Plants & Flowers
Ketchum, ID
208.726.7788
www.primaverasunvalley.com

The Picket Fence
Ketchum, ID
208.726.5511, 866.944.5511
www.thepicketfence.com

Sue Bridgman Florist
Ketchum, ID
208.725.0606
www.bridgmanflorist.com

Table Toppers Event Planners
Sun Valley, ID
208.578.0583
www.tabletoppersv.com

Taylor'd Events
Ketchum, ID
208.725.2027
www.taylordeventssv.com

That's Entertainment
Party Rentals
Ketchum, ID
208.726.8800
www.thatsentertainmentsv.com

Wine

*(Consider trying wines by any
of these vineyards who have
generously participated in the
Sun Valley Center Wine Auction)*

3 Horse Ranch Vineyards
Adelsheim Vineyards
Alexander Valley Vineyards
AmByth Estate
Andrew Will Winery
Anomaly Vineyards
Antinori
Araujo Estate Wines
Argyle Winery
Arkenstone Vineyards
Ascentia Wine Estates:
    Columbia Winery ·
Avanti Fine Wine Selections
Avventura Vintners
Axios
B.R. Cohn Winery
Barefoot Cellars
Barnett Vineyards
Basel Cellars Estate Winery
Beaucanon Estate
Bell Wine Cellars
Blackbird Vineyards
BOND
Bonterra Vineyards
Booker Vineyard
Brown Forman Wines
Buehler Vineyards
Buoncristiani Family Winery
Cadaretta Wines/Clayhouse Wines
CADE Winery
Cain Vineyard and Winery
Cakebread Cellars
Calera Wine Company
Camas Prairie Winery
Canihan Family Cellars
Cardinale
Carol Shelton Wines
Carter Cellars
Casa Piena
Castiglion del Bosco

Caymus Vineyards
Chalk Hill Estate Vineyards
    and Winery
Champagne Laurent-Perrier
Champagne Taittinger
Chappellet Vineyard
Charles Krug:
    Peter Mondavi Family
Charles Krug Winery
Chateau Boswell Winery
    and Jacquelynn Wines
Chateau Montelena Winery
Chateau Ste. Michelle
    Wine Estates
Cinder
Clendenen Family Vineyard
Clark-Claudon Vineyards
Cliff Lede Vineyards
Cline Cellars
Clos LaChance Wines
Clos Pegase Winery
Col Solare
Cold Springs Winery
Colgin Cellars
Colvin Winery
Concannon Vineyard
CONSTANT: Diamond Mountain
    Vineyard
Cornerstone Cellars
Corra Wines
Côte Bonneville
Covey Run Winery
D.R. Stephens Estate Wines
Darioush
David Arthur Vineyards
DeLille Cellars and Doyenne
Denner Vineyards
Dolce
Dom Pérignon
Domaine Napa Wine
Domaine Serene
Don Sebastiani and Sons
Donelan Family Wines
Dry Creek Vineyard
Duckhorn Wine Company
DuMOL Wine Co.
Dunham Cellars
Dunn Vineyards
E & J Gallo Winery
Egelhoff Wines
El Molino Winery
Elkhorn Ridge Vineyards
    and Winery
Epicurean Wines
Etude Wines
Fantesca Estate & Winery
Far Niente
Ferrari-Carano Vineyards
    and Winery
Ferreus Wines Inc.
Fidelitas
Figge Cellars
Fisher Vineyards
Five Star Cellars Inc.
Flora Springs Winery
    and Vineyards
Foley Estates Vineyard
    and Winery
Forgeron Cellars
Forman Vineyard
Frank Family Vineyards
Frenchman's Gulch Winery
Frogmore Creek
Gargiulo Vineyards
Gemstone Vineyard
George IV Wines
Gifford Hirlinger
Gramona
Grassi Wine Company
Grgich Hills Estate
HALL Wines
Halleck Vineyard
Hanzell Vineyards
Harris Estate Vineyards
Hartwell Vineyards
Hawkes Wine
HdV Wines

Hedges Family Estate
Heitz Wine Cellars
Hells Canyon Winery
Hightower Cellars
Honig Vineyard and Winery
hope and grace Winery
Hundred Acre
Hunt Cellars
Icon Estates, A Constellation
    Company
Il Borro
IO Wines
Ironstone Vineyards
J. Benton Furrow
J. Brut
J.P. Harbison Wines
Jack Creek Cellars
Jackson Family Wines and Verite
    Estate Winery
Jericho Canyon Vineyard
Joseph Phelps Vineyards
Judd's Hill Winery
JUSTIN Vineyards and Winery
K Vintners
Kelleher Family Vineyard
Kendall-Jackson Winery
KitFox Vineyards
Kristine Ashe Vineyards
Kuleto Estate
La Jota Vineyard Company
La Sirena Winery
Lachini Vineyards
Ladera Vineyards
Lail Vineyards
Lambert Bridge Winery
Landmark Vineyards
L'Aventure Winery
L'Ecole No. 41
Leonetti Cellar
Lindstrom Wine
Long Shadows Vintners
MacMurray Ranch Vineyards
Magito Wines
Matanzas Creek Winery
Matthews Estate
Melville Winery
Mercer Wine Estates
Merry Edwards Winery
Merryvale Vineyards
Meteor Vineyard
Michael David Winery
Michel-Schlumberger Wine Estate
Moet Hennessy USA
Mumm Napa
Napa Cellars
Neal Family Vineyards
Nicholas Cole Cellars
Northstar Winery
Oakville Ranch Vineyards
Opus One
O'Shaughnessy Estate Winery
Palmeri Wines
Paoletti Estates Winery
Paradigm Winery
Parallel Napa Valley
Parry Cellars
PATZ & HALL
Paul Hobbs Winery
Peay Vineyards
Peju Province Winery
Penner-Ash Wine Cellars
Pepper Bridge Winery
Pietra Santa Winery
Pillar Rock Vineyard
Pine Ridge Vineyards
Pisoni Vineyards and Winery
PlumpJack Winery
Pride Mountain Vineyards
Quilceda Creek Winery
Quinta do Tedo
R. Buoncristiani Vineyard, LLC
Ramey Wine Cellars
Ramian Estate
Rathbone Wine Group
Ravenswood Winery
Raymond Vineyards
Realm Cellars

Reeves Ranch Vineyard
Renwood Winery
Revana Family Vineyard
Reynolds Family Winery
Ridge Vineyards
Rivera Vineyards
Rivers-Marie Wines
Robert Foley Vineyards
Robert Mondavi Winery
Rombauer Vineyards
Round Pond Estate
Rubissow Wines
Rudd Winery
Rusack Vineyards
Saddleback Cellars
Saintsbury
Salvestrin Vineyards and Winery
Santa Lucia Highlands
Sawtooth Winery
Saxum Vineyards
Scarecrow Wine
Schramsberg Vineyards and
    J. Davies Vineyards
Schweiger Vineyards
Sebastiani Vineyards and Winery
Sequoia Grove Vineyards
Seven Hills Winery
Shafer Vineyards
Shaky Bridge
Sherwin Family Vineyards
SideJob Cellars
Siduri Winery
Silver Oak Cellars
Silverado Vineyards
Skipstone Estate
Sleight of Hand Cellars
Sloan Estate
Sokol Blosser Winery
Somerston Wine Co.
Sonador Cellars
Sonoma-Cutrer Vineyards
Spottswoode Estate Vineyard
    and Winery
Spring Mountain Vineyard
Spring Valley Vineyard
St. Supéry Vineyards and Winery
Stag's Leap Wine Cellars
Staglin Family Vineyard
Ste. Chapelle Winery
Stewart Cellars
Stolpman Vineyards
Sullivan Vineyards
SYZYGY
Talley Vineyards
Tamarack Cellars
Terra Valentine Winery
Terry Hoage Vineyards
The Hess Collection Winery
The Hogue Cellars
The Other Guys
Three Rivers Winery
Thurston Wolfe Winery
Toasted Head Winery
TOR Kenward Family Wines
Treana Winery
Trefethen Family Vineyards
Trinchero Family Estates
Va Piano Vineyards
Valley of the Moon Winery
Venge Vineyards
Venteux Vineyards
Villa Creek Cellars
Vina de Blanco
Vine One
Vineyard 29
Vineyard 7 and 8
Wente Vineyards
WesMar Winery
Whitehall Lane Winery
Whitman Cellars
William Hill Estate Winery
Wilson Daniels, Ltd.
Woodhouse Family Cellars
Woodward Canyon Winery
X Winery and Amicus Cellars
Zahtila Vineyards
ZD Wines

index